in partnership with:

THE VENTURE MENTORING TEAM

TheVMT.org

Copyright © 2021 by StartupBiz.com LLC

All rights reserved. Except for the sample forms and agreements, no part of this publication may be reproduced, distributed, or transmitted in any form or by any means, including photocopying, recording, or other electronic or mechanical methods, without the prior written permission of the publisher, except in the case of brief quotations embodied in critical reviews and certain other noncommercial uses permitted by copyright law.

For permission requests, please email mike@startupbiz.com.

ACTIONS AD RESOURCES FOR LAUNCHING A
VIABLE BUSINESS

Startup Stepping Stones

Disclaimer: StartupBiz.com LLC and its associates do not provide tax, legal or accounting advice. This material has been prepared for informational purposes only, and is not intended to provide, and should not be relied on for professional services. You should consult your own advisors before engaging in any transaction. Any services to be provided by StartupBiz.com LLC shall be governed by a separate agreement executed between the parties.

While we use reasonable efforts to furnish accurate and up-to-date information, we do not warrant that any information contained in this book is accurate, complete, reliable, current, or error-free. We assume no liability or responsibility for any errors or omissions in the content of this material.

This book is provided on an "as is" and "as available" basis. Use of this material is at your own risk. We disclaim all warranties. Neither we nor our associates shall be liable for any damages of any kind resulting from the use of this material or the actions undertaken by you or your advisors to start a business.

© StartupBiz.com LLC
Florida | USA
Phone 206-930-9121 • Email mike@startupbiz.com

Table of Contents

The Heart of the Start: A Personal Intro from the Author 3

How to Use This Guide 6

The Stepping Stones 8

    Validate the Idea 9

    Incorporate the Company 14

    Form the Team 18

    Conduct Primary Market Research 23

    Develop and Test Product Prototype 18

    Scrub Business Plan and Projections 23

    Secure Intellectual Property 26

    Create Name and Brand Strategy 31

    Outsource Ancillary Functions 35

    Draft Guerilla Marketing and Sales Plan 38

    Capitalize the Company 43

    Operate the Company 48

Bonus Templates 54

    Articles of Incorporation 55

    Company By-laws 57

    Limited Liability Company (LLC) Partnership Agreement 66

    Buy-Sell Agreement 80

    Work for Hire, Nondisclosure & Confidentiality Agreement . 84

    Executive Summary Format 89

    Intellectual Property Assignment Agreement 90

    Mutual Non-Disclosure Agreement 95

About the Author and VMT 99

The Heart of the Start: A Personal Introduction from the Author

Hey there! I'm Mike ODonnell. I'm honored to be your personal guide through this material. Thanks for giving this book a good read. I hope it becomes an indispensable guide on your journey.

There are literally thousands of great books, blogs, and articles on starting a business. There are more than 2,000 startup accelerators that teach it, and just about every college and university offers classes on entrepreneurship. 'How to Start a Business' is probably one of the most written and talked about subjects. We live in the golden age of entrepreneurship.

My purpose here is NOT to replicate that content. My purpose is to distill the heart of the start into easily digestible, bite sized chunks. This guide is designed to give you the actionable steps and supporting resources to make good decisions and get the RIGHT things DONE in the right ORDER. My purpose is to give you the nuggets and the best sources of additional information and tools.

After 30+ years of starting businesses and helping thousands of other aspiring entrepreneurs to launch their businesses, I've learned three critical things:

First, startup success does not happen in leaps and bounds. It happens in little hops. It's a series of **Stepping Stones**. You will find in this guide the important hops. Your job is to hop from one stone to the next, then to the next...and the next....until you find yourself in business. But not just any business. A viable business. There's a difference between starting a company and a viable business.

Read more about that here: The Difference Between Having a Company and a Business and How to Tell an Entrepreneur from a Wannapreneur.

Second, just about everything you need to launch a viable business has been created. Just reach out and take them. Leverage the knowledge, tools, and short cuts that others have already blazed for you. Too many first-time entrepreneurs try to go it alone and reinvent the wheel. I've assembled for you herein the links to many of those resources. Take a deep dive off the steps you need more help with. Surface, then take the next step.

Third, the single biggest MISTAKE most first-time entrepreneurs make is working on the wrong things in the wrong order. They don't focus on the most important and immediate next step. They try to jump too far ahead. They waste time, money, and energy on the wrong tasks. This guide presents the right steps in the right order.

Read more about how to do that here: The Startup Founder Imperative: Balancing the Important with the Immediate

In this process, don't try to fake it. Don't try to pretend you know more than you do. It's okay to: Admit It, You Don't Have a Clue What You're Doing.

There are many other lessons you can leverage to make these hops, like these: 19 Lessons from 19 Years Working with Startups. This guide tries to touch on the most important ones.

Finally, I would be remiss if I didn't define what it means to launch a *viable business*. The definition will differ depending on the size and scope of the startup. A scalable startup planning to raise millions of dollars to serve a global market, will have different requirements than a self-funded lifestyle business serving a local market.

In this guide, launching a viable business means introducing a product or service that people want or need, with a competitive advantage in a market that is large enough to generate profitability, and promises to be sustainable and worth the effort for its founders and employees.

My greatest hope for this guide is that you use it over-and-over again. Look, many startup ideas don't work out. That's fine. Most successful entrepreneurs had several failures before hitting on the one that took off. I am hoping you find this guide just as valuable when you start your second and third business, as you do for the first. Enjoy the journey!

How to Use This Guide

This guide is comprised of twelve Stepping Stones. Completing the steps guarantees a successful launch of a viable business. Whether the business grows and thrives after launch requires a whole different set of steps. Think of these first steps as foundational stones.

In one respect, each stone is a sequential step in starting a company. There is no need to form a company until you have validated the idea; no need to secure the intellectual property until you have conducted primary research, developed a prototype, and scrubbed the business plan. When you land on Step 11, you are well on your way to having a viable business.

If you have already completed some of these steps, feel free to skip ahead, but review the suggestions to make sure you haven't missed anything. Like the cornerstones of a solid foundation, each step in starting a viable business is built upon the ones before it.

Each Stepping Stone begins with a verb, i.e., *validate, form, conduct, develop, create*, etc. This is to reinforce that you are moving from simulation to reality, from learning and thinking to planning and action. After all the thinking and planning, the thing that matters most is what you **DO** to advance your idea and turn it into a viable business.

Each step is broken down into five teachings:

Quote: Sage advice from experts to reinforce the importance of the step.

Introduction: Offers some advice based on years of real-world experience. It sets the stage for what you should think about, decide, and then do.

Things to Think About and Decide: Offers suggestions on how to take the step. Think, Decide, Do.

Things to Do and Avoid: Offers a list of tasks and common traps to avoid. Also covers some best practices you may not have thought about.

Recommended Readings and Resources: Offers links to best-in-class books, tools, templates, web sites, and services that can help you start and build your business.

This is the real value of this guide. These are your short cuts. Mix and match the readings and resources to create your personal blueprint for success.

NOTE: If you got the paperback version of this book, rather than the ebook, you can get a free copy of the digital version with hyperlinks to all of the resources. Simply post a review of this book on Amazon and then request the free ebook by sending an email to:

startupsteppingstones@startupbiz.com

You will receive the ebook by return email in PDF format with active hyperlinks.

The Stepping Stones

 12. Operate

 11. Capitalize

 10. Draft

 9. Outsource

 8. Create

 7. Secure

 6. Scrub

 5. Develop

 4. Conduct

 3. Form

 2. Incorporate

 1. Validate

Validate the Idea

"Here's the difference between a visionary and an entrepreneur. Both have visions, which are a dime a dozen. But an entrepreneur has, in addition to visions, plans. In addition to plans, actions."

– Bob Metcalfe, Founder of 3Com and inventor of Ethernet

You should start by doing (or finishing) the groundwork necessary to validate the business opportunity. Every business idea, no matter how good, depends on how well it is developed and ultimately transformed into a money-making venture.

How do you know how good your idea is? It starts with an inspiration. It is fueled by passion. It becomes a reality only with hard work and persistence. An idea is fickle. It will tease you, seduce you, and even deceive you. Before you devote a significant portion of your life to it, be sure it will be worth it…. even if it does not succeed… because it may not.

Contrary to common perception, whether or not your idea can be transformed into a sustainable business, is not entirely within your control. There are too many variables and unforeseen challenges to predict. Good ideas fail, even with sufficient resources and flawless execution.

If you can't afford to fail, financially or emotionally, don't start. If you know in your heart that starting a business will bring you closer to your dreams and goals even if this business fails, then proceed with gusto. But first, do your homework and do everything in your power to mitigate your risks.

Along the way, be receptive to new insights and serendipity, then adjust your course accordingly. This is called "the pivot." Most successful businesses end up being very different than what they started out to be.

As you begin this journey, there are some things to think about, things to decide, and things to do that will increase your odds of a favorable outcome.

Things to Think About and Decide

First, do not proceed to form a company unless you are truly passionate about the idea and have validated it with real customers. Your motivation should be more than just money. You should also be motivated by the possibility of making a difference, creating something new (or better), and the opportunity to learn and grow. Remember that people do not buy ideas. They buy products and services that solve a problem or fulfill a need. You should list the data points that are required to validate that your idea can be transformed into a money-making product.

Second, think about your idea as a "project," or an "experiment," not as a business. Once the project achieves certain milestones (see below), you can turn it into a business. Many people will tell you to "focus, focus, focus" on one idea. That's actually bad advice. It is okay to try lots of different ideas until one sticks -- until it keeps you up at night and forces you to do nothing but it. The right idea will find you. You will know you have the right idea when your enthusiasm is not driven solely by your love for the idea, but by the love for the idea from people who will buy it.

Third, decide how much time and money you can devote to the idea. Decide what must happen and by when for it to continue. Decide what would kill the idea, for you to cut your losses and move on to another idea. If you have a job, don't quit it until your idea becomes a business capable of generating revenue within a timeframe that does not burn up all your savings, or at least until the business can attract outside investors.

Fourth, think about whether the idea translates into a lifestyle company, or a high-growth company. They have very different requirements. Can the eventual product scale? Can it be replicated and sold on a mass scale, or is it limited by geography or number of units that can be produced? There is no right or wrong answer in terms of the size of the business opportunity. There is only what is right for you and your ability to attract enough customers to create a profitable business.

Fifth, think about how to simplify the idea. Too much must happen before anything can happen, so the simpler it is, the more likely it can be done. If your idea requires a lot of complexity or ongoing customizations to serve the market, think hard about its viability and your ability to make it happen.

Sixth, decide on the THING that makes it unique or better and be able to articulate that within 15 seconds. What's your "secret sauce" or "sweet spot?" What is the one THING that customers will absolutely LOVE about the product? What is the pain point you are addressing? Why hasn't anyone else brought it to market? What gives you a competitive advantage?

Seventh, decide on ONE revenue stream. Use that to guide exactly what it is you are building and in what order. Think about your ability to build the product and bring it to market without any outside capital. Do you have the capital, or access to friends and family capital? Most investors don't invest in ideas or to build product, they invest in traction and growth -- traction with paying customers and growth in sales and profits.

Eighth, think about joining a startup accelerator. Checkout GAN.

Things to Do and Avoid

Collect and organize data on the market, competitive solutions, and product development costs. Figure out who is *really* going to buy it and how much they will pay for it.

Organize an informal working group of friends and colleagues to be your sounding board. Seek out as many different perspectives on the idea and the potential business, as you possibly can.

Do not worry about people stealing your idea. That is the sign of an amateur. If the idea is that easy for anyone to steal and implement – it offers no barriers to entry – it's probably not worth doing.

Develop a one-minute pitch that clearly articulates the product, the market size and need, and your unique advantage.

Develop a non-functional model of the product that you can show people. This can be an illustration, PowerPoint presentation, or other visual.

Survey potential users of the product. Have them rank in order the features that are most important to them.

Set up daily Google Alerts for keywords that describe your solution and market. Read as much as you can about how customers are currently solving the problem your solution proposes to solve, and what they are paying for it.

Follow blogs that cover your market. Checkout Flippa, BetaBound, ProductHunt, and other new product listing services to see if there are similar sites on the market as the one you have in mind. You might even be able to buy one in beta real cheap, or private label it, to get a head start!

Search the Apple, Android, and Amazon App Stores to see if there are similar apps or solutions as the one you have in mind. Your solution can't be just a little better, cheaper, or faster. It needs to be at least FIVE times better – preferably 10 times better.

Recommended Readings and Resources

The Value Proposition, Harvard Labs
Excellent video on how to nail the value proposition.

[Will It Fly? How to Test Your Next Business Idea So You Don't Waste Your Time and Money,](#) by Pat Flynn

[Idea Evaluation Checklist,](#) by Entrepreneur Magazine

[How to Start a Startup,](#) by Paul Graham

[The Four Steps to the Epiphany: Successful Strategies for Products that Win,](#) by Steven Blank

[The Path to Starting A Startup,](#) by Scott Weiss, TechCrunch

[How to Build a Startup,](#) by Steve Blank Course on Udacity Course

[Is Your Idea Any Good?](#) by Mike ODonnell, StartupBiz.com

[Minimum Viable Company: A simple way to develop and pitch your next company,](#) by T.A. McCann

[Evernote](#) or [OneNote](#)
Make notes, sync between your computer, phone, and tablet. Collaborate with co-founders.

[Startup Genome](#)
Score your readiness and likeliness of success. Track your progress as you develop and grow your startup.

[The Heart of the Start: Falling in Love with the Right Idea,](#) by Mike ODonnell, Startupbiz.com

[What's the Risk Someone Will Steal Your Startup Idea?](#) By Mike ODonnell, StartupBiz.com

[Trajectory: Startup: Ideation to Product/Market Fit,](#) by Dave Parker

Incorporate the Company

"The only thing worse than starting something and failing… is not starting something."

—Seth Godin, Dotcom Business Executive, Author and Blogger

Even though you may still be in the idea stage and not yet sure whether the opportunity you have identified can be turned into a viable business, you should form a legal entity if you plan to pursue it. A legally formed company affords you and your idea protections that are not available to you as an individual. Most startup companies are corporations, not sole proprietorships. A corporation limits shareholder liability. It's a repository for intellectual property and other assets. Perhaps most importantly, a corporate entity provides a vehicle for inbound investment.

The first thing to come to grips with is that YOU are not your company. Your company is a creature of the law. Your company has a life of its own. It wants to survive, and it wants to protect itself, even from you. What is best for your company is not necessarily best for you. The role you play determines your obligations and your liability. As an officer and/or director of your startup company, the law will hold you accountable. And the minute you hire someone, or take investment money from someone, or enter into a business contract with someone, your obligations and liabilities increase exponentially.

Things to Think About and Decide

First, think about the costs, advantages, disadvantages, and tax consequences of the different types of legal entities.

Second, decide which legal form your company should take:

"C" Corp

- ✓ Common choice for growth companies.
- ✓ No limitations on foreign or entity shareholders.
- ✓ Ability to issue multiple classes and series of stock.
- ✓ Earnings are subject to taxation once at the corporate level, and once at the stockholder level.
- ✓ Best choice for companies planning to raise money from institutional investors.

"S" Corp

- ✓ Potentially beneficial to prefunded companies or bootstrapped companies.
- ✓ Profits and losses "pass through" to shareholders.
- ✓ Ownership limitations prohibit non-U.S. shareholders and most entity shareholders.
- ✓ Multiple classes of stock are prohibited.

"LLC"

- ✓ Potentially beneficial to startups in the idea validation and testing stage, when the likelihood of continuing to develop the product is uncertain.
- ✓ Profits and losses "pass through" to equity owners.
- ✓ No restriction on foreign or entity ownership.
- ✓ Costly to implement multiple classes of equity.
- ✓ Costly to implement equity incentive plans.
- ✓ Lots of tax issues.
- ✓ Most professional investors avoid LLCs.
- ✓ Generally, not recommended for growth companies, but may be suitable for a startup, with a path to migrate to a "C" Corp if and when the business opportunity is proved out.

Third, decide on the jurisdiction to incorporate. Most "C" corps choose Delaware because it is familiar to investors nationwide, has well defined and tested corporate law, and is fast and efficient. The downside to incorporating in Delaware is a higher formation and maintenance expense and carries a potentially large annual franchise tax. If you need to start quickly and cost-effectively, forming an LLC in your state might be fine to secure immediate corporate benefits.

Things to Do and Avoid

Do not proceed to invest time, money, and other resources to develop a business as a sole proprietor. Invest in the appropriate legal structure if you plan to build a business that will have other founders, employees and/or investors.

Seek the advice of a good corporate attorney to decide which type of business entity you should form.

When putting together your board of directors, make sure to have an odd number to avoid voting and policy stalemates.

Register for a [fictitious name](#) in your home state.

File an annual corporate report and obtain the proper licenses for the type of business being operated, as required by your state.

Visit the Secretary of State website for a detailed list of applications, licensing, and compliance requirements.

Get an Employee Identification Number (EIN) from the IRS to open a bank account and to file your tax return each year — even if you have no revenues or do not plan to have a profit.

Set up a reminder system for all state and federal tax, licensing, reporting, filing and compliance requirements.

Recommended Readings and Resources

Steps to Starting a Small Business The Company Corporation

LegalZoom, Templates, services, and legal assistance for starting a company.

The Startup Company Lawyer by Yokum Taku

FindLaw
A leading database of resources regarding legal issues from finding lawyers to researching rules and finding legal forms.

Templates: **Articles of Incorporation, Company By-Laws, and LLC Partnership Agreement,** StartupBiz.com Templates.

Application for Employer Identification Number (EIN) Internal Revenue Service

Form the Team

"You need three things to create a successful startup: to start with good people, to make something customers actually want, and to spend as little money as possible."

— *Paul Graham*

Most startups will rise or fall based on the quality of their teams. Few things cause a startup to implode faster than infighting among the founders or a dysfunctional team. Most venture capitalists invest more on the strength of the team than on any other factor. It is often said among investors, "We bet on the jockey, not on the horse." If you have a great horse (idea), but you are not a skilled jockey (CEO), don't be afraid to give up the reins and find a partner who can take you to the finish line.

How many founders should a startup team have? Studies show that two founders are ideal. Famous founder duos include Hewlett-Packard (HP), Gates-Allen (Microsoft), Lerner-Bosack (Cisco), and Jobs-Wozniak (Apple). With duos, one is usually good at business development and the other good at product development. There are many good examples of sole founders and triad founders, but precious few good examples of four or more founders. There is no magic number, but there is magic to building a great team around the founder(s).

If you're a solo founder, that's okay, but you are still going to need to recruit a great team. The notion of the entrepreneur as lone wolf or soaring eagle is a myth. Bill Gates, the iconic founder of Microsoft, once said that the secret to his success was that he hired people smarter than himself.

Almost nothing you do from this point forward will be more important than assembling (and keeping) the core team -- especially the people who will drive sales, product development and operations.

What does it mean to "form" the core team? It means the business must have a Founders Agreement, Founder / Shareholder Buy-Sell Agreement, Stock Vesting Agreement and Schedule, and other legal instruments that institutionalize the role, responsibilities, and compensation of the core team. (Templates for most of these docs can be found on StartupBiz.com.)

Many startups have failed or suffered serious setbacks because the founders and/or core team operated on a handshake or weak organizational and management documents.

Your founder documents should clearly address what happens upon any of the three dreaded D's: Death, Debt, and Divorce. What happens if a founder dies? What happens if a founder declares personal bankruptcy or incurs debt that forces him/her to sell his/her stock? What happens when a founder gets divorced, or if one founder wants to "separate" from the other?

Things to Think About and Decide

First, if you do not already have a co-founder, think long and hard about whether you really need one. Think about what experience and skills your co-founder(s) should have to compliment your experience and skills. It rarely works when both founders want to do the same type of work.

Second, think about how you will create a positive culture that matches your outlook and personality? A culture cannot be manufactured. It must be an extension of the character of the leaders and their core values.

Third, if your startup has more than one founder, decide who will be the "boss". A company needs a CEO. It rarely works for a company to have two CEOs who have equal decision-making authority.

Fourth, decide how much equity each founder will start with based on his or her contribution of (1) money or in-kind contributions (equipment, office, space, etc.), (2) expertise (know-how) or intellectual property (invention) and (3) deliverables (what they do for the business, not what they say they will do).

Fifth, decide over what period of time each founder will vest his or her shares. The industry standard is vesting over four (4) years, unless a company is sold before then. NEVER give any founder a significant number of shares upfront, just because he or she was present at the start. It is what each founder contributes to the success of the business in the long run that counts most.

Things to Do and Avoid

Hire EVERYONE on contract for at least 90 days before hiring as W2 employee.

Have a Buy-Sell agreement among the founders. Do not simply issue shares to the founders. Vest shares over four years for performance and measurable metrics that are commensurate with each founder's contribution to the business.

Never-EVER issue stock 50/50 among founders. If two founders have an equal percentage, grant a tie-breaking percentage to a trusted advisor. Set clear milestones and expectations among all team members.

Have all founders and employees sign an Intellectual Property (IP) Assignment Agreement.

Don't hire a professional CEO or head of sales right out of the gate. Be the CEO or find a co-founder capable of being CEO. The founder/CEO needs to be the head of sales until the company reaches breakeven, or until it has achieved key performance milestones that attracts ongoing customer accounts and/or outside financing.

Hire everyone based on the three-way test: 1) Can s/he do the job (competency)? 2) Will s/he do the job (capability)? 3) Can we stand to work with her or him as s/he does the job (chemistry)?

Research related job postings from similar companies and write job descriptions that include a compelling business vision, clear description of each role you need to hire, and list of critical skills. Do this for every key role you need now or in the future. Read them weekly, post them to friends and on job boards. This exercise keeps you focused on "who" you must have to eventually succeed.

Develop a thorough interview process for every key role that includes phone screening, face-to-face interviewing, interview questions, background checks, peer reviews, and test projects. (Read the book Who: The A Method for Hiring.)

Identify credible domain experts in your field or in one of the key areas of your product development and invite three of them to meet you via Google Hangout or Skype. During the conversation, explain your vision and request if you can speak again to get feedback on your approach. Repeat this process until you find three or four domain experts willing to join your board of advisors.

Allocate about 15% of the company's common stock to a stock option pool and issue key employees options which vest over 3-4 years.

Create a board of advisors and draft an equity compensation plan and meeting schedule for the advisors. Allocate and issue approximately 0.25% of company stock to each advisor, to be vested over a 2–3-year period.

Recommended Readings and Resources:

[The 10 Most Serious Hiring Mistakes and How to Fix Them](#) by Brad Smart

[What to Look for in Job Candidates When Hiring for Your Startup](#) by Mike ODonnell

[The Art of Recruiting](#) by Guy Kawasaki

[Framework for Paying Startup Team Contributors in Stock](#) by Mike ODonnell, StartupBiz.com

[How to Pick a Co-Founder](#) Venture Hacks

[Stop Looking for a Co-Founder](#) by Dave Lerner

[The Perils of Founder Fighting](#) by Mark Suster

[Choosing a Co-Founder: Three Mistakes to Avoid](#) by OpenView

[TopGrading](#) by Bradford Smart

[Anticipating the Dreaded Three D's that Derail Startup Founders and Business Owners](#) by Mike ODonnell

[Startup Team Symmetry](#) by Mike ODonnell, StartupBiz.com

[Entrepreneurial DNA](#) by Bosi Profile

[Co-Founders Lab](#)
Search for a potential co-founder; review profiles of available people; attend matchmaking events.

[Three Criteria for High-Performing Teams](#), by Mike ODonnell, StartupBiz.com

[Would I Ride into Startup Battle with You?](#) by Mike ODonnell

Conduct Primary Market Research

*"The golden rule for every businessman is this:
Put yourself in your customer's place."*

– Orison Swett Marden, Founder, SUCCESS Magazine, Author

You have probably done a fair amount of secondary market research on your idea. It's one thing to collect data on your market by doing some secondary research, but you must really "know" your target customers by doing primary research. The only way to do that is to get face-to-face with them and LET THEM DO MOST OF THE TALKING. You should learn everything about your market — your customers and your competition — that can possibly be learned.

Hopefully, YOU are part of the target market. You would love the product, buy the product, and tell everyone you know about it even if it was not yours! With a little luck, the fact you understand the market so well has given you a unique insight into why your idea can be transformed into a money-making machine.

The goal of primary market research is to discover the answers to, and craft a crystal-clear description of, the five W's:

Who is the paying customer, exactly? *What* motivates them to purchase your product? *Where* are they likely to purchase your product? *When* are they likely to purchase your product? *Why* would they purchase your product over other solutions?

As a bonus, you should also be able to address the *How's*: How are they likely to find out about it and how much will they pay for it?

Simple questions, yes, but super hard to answer without digging deeply into the needs, wants, and pain points of the customer.

Things to Think About and Decide

First, decide what segment of the market you should serve first. Your product likely has multiple applications and features for multiple markets. You must make hard choices about which one to pursue first. Find the segment ripe for disruption (the opportunity) and identify the customer's sweet spot (the burning need) within that segment.

Second, determine the size of the addressable market. Is it big enough? Is it growing or shrinking?

Third, profile the "typical" customer by demographics, geographics, and psychographics. What are the other characteristics of your target market and how does your solution fit these characteristics?

Fourth, identify the competitors – or the solutions customers currently use to solve the problem your product proposes to solve. What share of the market do these solutions have? Can you grab some of this share, or do you plan to grab new share as the market grows?

Fifth, specifically define your special insight into the needs, behaviors, or trends of the market that others do not have. Is this market really where you want to spend the next five to ten years of your life?

Things to Do and Avoid

Read the book Nail It then Scale It: The Entrepreneur's Guide to Creating and Managing Breakthrough Innovation. Use it to create a process and plan for conducting primary market research.

Estimate the annual revenues generated by the total addressable market (TAM), the service addressable market

(SAM) and your target market (TM) segment for your solution. Produce one "top down" revenue figure by finding key market research and produce a second "bottom up" revenue figure by estimating the number of users or buyers, the average price, and the average amount spent on purchases per year.

Find (and If necessary, purchase) a recent research report on your market by a reputable research vendor.

Summarize your market: (1) How old is the market? (2) How many companies (or consumers) are in the market? (3) How many people work in the field? (4) How large is the market in terms of annual revenues and number of units sold? (5) Who are the chief competitors and which ones have gone public or sold in the last three years?

List the top two or three conferences for the industry and try to watch videos of the events, attend a webinar, or attend a conference in person.

Read the websites, online information, and sales presentations of the top three competitors in your market. Hint: check Scribd, YouTube and Slideshare.

Survey your target market using Mechanical Turk or SurveyMonkey.

Create a User Persona that describes the wants/needs of your typical customer; how this customer learns about your product, and how this customer goes about buying and using your product.

Run a mini ad campaign on Google AdWords, Facebook, and/or Linkedin using keywords that describe your target market, to collect click-thru data. Find out what other companies are paying to dominate those keywords.

Recommended Readings & Resources

Performing Critical #Startup Research on the Cheap Video by Dan Shapiro

Startup Market Research (video) Market Research for Startups (slides) by Kirk Burton

Customer Development is Not a Focus Group by Steve Blank

Startup Metrics by Dave McClure

CrunchBase
Free database of technology companies, people, and investors. Good place to see if a company is already doing what you are thinking of doing. Good place to learn where investors are placing their bets and which ones might be interested in your deal. See who has invested in your competitors.

IBISworld
Industry and market research reports.

Miscellaneous Market Research Sources:

Gartner Group	Klue	Internet Archive
Forrester Group	Quantcast.com	Labor Statistics
eMarketer	Alexa	

Develop and Test Product Prototype

"If you are not embarrassed by the first version of your product, you've launched too late."

~ Reid Hoffman, co-founder of PayPal and LinkedIn

This is where the rubber meets the road in terms of customer validation and market traction.

Nothing succeeds faster than a functional product… or at least a good visual representation of the product you want to build. The quicker you can develop a prototype and show it to prospective customers, the sooner you can collect the feedback necessary to build a Minimum Viable Product (MVP).

There is so much good know-how information, and so many good tools available for building a minimum viable product, there is no excuse for wasting time and money on building a product that no one wants. There is an entire cottage industry dedicated to inexpensive and rapid product development.

Product prototyping and development is a six-step process:

1. Collect product, market, and competitive data (with an emphasis on primary market research), to validate the "sweet spot" of your product.

2. Brainstorm features and focus on the one or two critical features that customers want most.

3. Develop a prototype – even if it is a paper mockup.

4. Test the prototype with target customers.

5. Measure the customer feedback; rinse and repeat until you have a product specification that customers love.

6. Build the *real* product on a rapid development schedule and get it into the hands of customers for further testing and refinement.

Things to Think About and Decide

First, think about the key value proposition of your product.

Second, think about the key metrics needed to determine whether your product is valuable to users and whether it is getting traction.

Third, decide on the <u>least</u> amount of functionality you need to have to test the product with real customers?

Fourth, determine what skills you need to have or source to build a Minimum Viable Product.

Fifth, think about the fastest and least expensive method and tools at your disposal to create a functional prototype.

Things to Do and Avoid

Create a [use case](#) and a [user persona](#) for your product. Validate it with actual users.

Write one paragraph describing the entire offering that you are trying to create or have created. Write at least fifteen different key "Features" that your offering needs to have at launch.

Arrange the "Features" into logical "Groups," and sort the "Features" by placing the most important "Features" at the top of the "Group" list and the less important ones at the bottom.

Order the "Groups" by placing the most important "Groups" first, building a basic "Development Roadmap." Eliminate any less important "Features."

Organize "Features" in the most important "Groups" into releases and identify your first minimum viable product ("MVP") release that is simple. See http://fndri.com/yVKzvp as a template.

Write two sentences describing each "Group" and two sentences on the key "Features" in your MVP, and provide a strategy and time estimate to develop each "Feature."

Use basic prototyping tools, such as Balsamiq or Protoshare to develop a non-functional mockup of your MVP.

Develop a proposal for an aggressive two-week product development sprint to complete a series of key features.

Launch a professionally designed landing page on your domain that states your vision and collects email addresses of interested customers or users. Alternatively, use https://www.launchrock.com/

Sign up for Microsoft BizSpark, Amazon AWS, or Google for Entrepreneurs to access development tools and services.

Depending on the complexity of your product, write a detailed product specification.

Recommended Readings & Resources

The Four Steps to the Epiphany by Steve Blank

Product Design and Development
by Karl Ulrich – The book presents a set of product development techniques aimed at bringing together the marketing, design, and manufacturing functions of the enterprise.

Lean Startup Methodologies by Eric Ries
Nail it then Scale It

Best-selling book on creating a product that people love and want to buy.

Database Design for Mere Mortals
by Michael Hernandez – Explains the technique of using sentence subjects to build a database model outlined.

How to Bring a Product to Market
by Venture Hacks – Nivi interviews Sean Ellis on how to get to product/market fit, how to measure fit, and how to survey your users so you can improve fit.

Squarespace
A fully hosted, completely managed environment for creating and maintaining a website with mobile-ready template designs.

SnapPages
Website creation tool.

Mockingbird
A web-based wireframing tool.

Figma, interface design tool.

FireFox Development Tools
Web development tool, integrates with Firefox. Edit, debug, and monitor CSS, HTML, and JavaScript live in any web page.

Basecamp, Mantis and Pivotal Tracker
Low-cost project management and bug tracking applications.

Google Analytics
A must-have tool for websites.

Google Developers
Developer tools, API's and technologies.

[Google Webmaster Tools](#) Optimize your website.

[Building a Minimum Viable Product](#) Video, by David Meadows

[Product Building and Innovation](#) Video, by Mike ODonnell

[Getting from Proof-of-Concept to Minimum Viable Product](#), Mike ODonnell, StartupBiz.com

Scrub Business Plan and Projections

"Plans are useless, but planning is indispensable."

~ President Dwight D. Eisenhower

Developing a clear path to profitability — and being able to defend it with good metrics — is probably the single most important thing a startup founder needs to do before launching a company — and certainly before meeting with investors. Sure, there are examples of successful startups (like Google and Pinterest) that did not know how they were going to make money before building their products, but those examples are rare. It is a far better strategy to build your product around a revenue stream, than to try and figure out how you will make money later.

Most startups make the mistake of pursuing multiple markets and multiple revenue streams. Successful startups focus on one revenue stream and perfect it before attempting to bring on additional revenue streams. Cash flow plus growth equals value. A good startup will focus on getting a large share of one market before diluting its resources to pursue multiple markets. Once your revenue model is crystallized, the task is to articulate it in a plan and detail it with a realistic set of financial projections.

Things to Think About and Decide

First, think about your primary revenue model. How do you plan to make money? Decide on ONE revenue stream to start. Model the cash flow with a basic [Pro forma](#).

Second, decide on the key assumptions and data points that support your financial projections. Think about what you need to show to defend your revenue model.

Third, think about the top-line assumptions, i.e., traffic, hits, conversion rates, price, churn, customer retention rates, etc. Think about your selling costs and the costs of running the business. Think about how these might change as you grow.

Fourth, decide how many customers you have to sell each month and at one average price point, to cash flow the business.

Things to Do and Avoid

Depending on the complexity of your product, write a detailed product specification.

Develop a realistic and defensible financial model, based on one revenue stream.

Describe in detail the steps that are required from the very beginning of the customer relationship to when a payment is received.

Detail your assumptions for expenses, such as fixed expenses and costs of goods sold, and how they will scale as the business grows.

Try to keep all costs variable. Do not take on fixed, long-term expenses unless your business absolutely requires it.

Set up your Chart of Accounts using Quick Books online or similar application.

Write an Executive Summary that includes how you will make money and how much money you need to reach break-even.

Don't write a business plan that is more than 50 pages, including financials. No one is likely to read it, least of all your own team.

Don't overly focus on product margins; focus on top-line revenues.

Prepare 3-5-year financial projections, with the first year showing revenues and expenses monthly, then quarterly for years 2-5.

Do NOT show "hockey stick" revenue projections, where the revenue is flat lined in year one, shows a modest increase in year two, then inexplicable soars in year three.

Have good answers (contingencies, fallback position) for what happens when things don't go according to plan (because they won't).

Recommended Readings & Resources

[Model Executive Summary Template](#)
by Mike ODonnell, StartupBiz.com

[Business Plan Template](#) StartupBiz.com

[Spreadsheet Template Download](#)
by Aaron Patzer of Mint.com via Founder Institute

[Sample Business Plans](#) and [Business Planning Software](#)
Bplans, Palo Alto Software

[Both Sides of the Table](#)
by Marc Suster – A blog that covers financial and business topics.

[Startup Business Models](#) by Dave Parker

[Startup Financial Models](#) by Dave Parker

[eCommerce Business Models](#) by Shyna Jain

[Business Model Examples](#) by Board of Innovation

[Business Model Canvas](#)
The Business Model Canvas, is a strategic management and entrepreneurial tool. It allows you to describe, design, challenge, invent, and pivot your business model.

Secure Intellectual Property

> *"If you didn't have patents, no one would bother to spend money on research and development. But with patents, if someone has a good idea and a competitor can't copy it, then that competitor will have to think of their own way of doing it. So then, instead of just one innovator, you have two or three people trying to do something in a new way."*
>
> *- James Dyson, Inventor*

It is never too soon to determine which protections you need and secure the necessary rights for your company.

Intellectual Property (IP) provides your startup with both an offense and a defense. It can create barriers to entry, increase the value of your company, attract investors, generate revenue through licensing and royalties, and reduce shareholder risk. There are many strategies for building a strong IP portfolio, from state and federal registrations, to assignment and confidentiality agreements.

Whether you should file patents or trademarks depends on the novelty of your idea, your branding strategy, and your budget. Even if you do not formally file for these protections, you should take care to guard the IP of your startup. Many companies have prospered not by filing, but by guarding their trade secrets and having airtight agreements with contributors. A good rule of thumb is to ensure that everyone who is contributing anything to your company, including yourself, has assigned those contributions to the company in writing and has agreed to keep them confidential.

Things to Think About and Decide

First, considering buying or licensing the patents for a product that was never commercialized. Tons of patents exist for products that were never built. Check the USPTO. You might be able to acquire one cheap!

Second, if you have a unique invention or technology, think about whether you should file a [provisional patent application](#) (they are quick and inexpensive relative to regular patent applications).

Third, if you plan to pursue a patent license from a university, think about whether you can demonstrate a thorough understanding of the product, the market, the developmental milestones, and the financial requirements to commercialize the technology with a reasonable probability of success.

Fourth, if you plan to pursue a patent license, think about whether you have the money, the legal counsel, and the patience to negotiate the license, which can often take 1-3 years.

Fifth, think about whether you should file a U.S. (and possibly international) trademark on your name, slogan, and/or logo.

Sixth, think about how you can protect your domain name from squatters.

Seventh, decide whether it might be more beneficial to protect your intellectual property with trade secrets and confidentiality agreements, instead of patent and copyright filings.

Eighth, think about recruiting an IP attorney for your board of advisors.

Things to Do and Avoid

Do not approach a university or federal agency that holds patent rights unless you have the necessary credentials to commercially develop the technology and attract financing.

Before approaching a patent holder, find out if the inventor is available. (It is rare that a technology can be commercialized without further input of the inventor(s). A good working relationship with the inventor(s) is necessary if you expect to succeed.)

If you decide to pursue a patent license, request a basic term sheet from the patent holder.

Conduct a preliminary patent search on the technology you plan to develop as a business. https://www.uspto.gov/patents/search.

Conduct a preliminary trademark search on names and/or marks you are thinking about using
https://www.uspto.gov/trademarks/search

Research best of breed templates and download (1) a Mutual Non-Disclosure Agreement for partners, (2) an Intellectual Property Assignment Agreement for team members, (3) a Work for Hire Agreement for development resources that properly assigns the Intellectual Property and (4) an Advisor Agreement that grants equity in exchange for high-level guidance. (Many of these templates are available for free on StartupBiz.com).

Mark all of your work products with a copyright notice and mark any sensitive information with the label "Confidential Information."

Ensure that everyone that you have worked with to develop the product has signed or will sign an Agreement with Intellectual Property Assignment.

Read every agreement you are asked to sign thoroughly. Have an attorney review and advise you on all key contracts.

Recommended Readings & Resources

Startup Company Intellectual Property Video by Jon Gibbons, Patent Attorney

Startup Legal Issues
Video by Brent Britton, GreyRobinson

Patent It Yourself
by David Pressman (available through Amazon.com)

Google Patent Search
Searches patent database for relevant patents.

USPTO
Patent and trademark research resource.

Patent Law Essentials
Patent law for business people.

Nolo
Forms and templates for trademarks, provisional patents, and other common tasks.

Trademarkia
Trademark search engine and filing service.

Tech Transfer Central
A one-stop source for information, news, products, and services for technology transfer and intellectual property professionals.

TechFinder, Michigan

NASA Technology Transfer Portal

Association of University Technology Managers
AUTM Global Technology Portal, where you can easily find the

latest university technologies available for licensing worldwide.

[The Startup Company Lawyer](#) by Yokum Taku

[StartupBiz.com](#)
Legal and business templates for startup companies.

[Justia](#)
Legal resources (Federal District Court Filings and Dockets).

[FindLaw](#)
A leading database of resources regarding legal issues from finding lawyers to researching rules and finding legal forms.

[PACER](#)
Access to online public court documents.

Create Name and Brand Strategy

> *"In this ever-changing society, the most powerful and enduring brands are built from the heart. They are real and sustainable. Their foundations are stronger because they are built with the strength of the human spirit, not an ad campaign. The companies that are lasting are those that are authentic."*
>
> — Howard Schultz, CEO of Starbucks

A name – and more importantly, a brand – gives life to a product and company. Everything in life has a perception about it. So, will it be for your product and your company. A name is what you are called. A brand is the identity — the positioning and points of differentiation — that your name is known for. A distinctive name combined with a good branding strategy allows you to create a wonderful impression about your product in the hearts and minds of your customers.

To win in the marketplace, it comes down to what people **"feel"** about your product, not what they "think" about your product. Your name does not have to appeal to everyone. Trying to promote a name that appeals to everyone is a bad strategy. Pick a name that you can build equity in and that you can defend from companies in the market and from potential squatters. Then build a brand around that name that communicates why you are a different and better choice than the other products in the market.

Things to Think About and Decide

First, think about making your company name and product name one in the same. It is very difficult (and expensive) for a startup to promote both a company name and a product name. Most people remember products, not companies (unless the companies are trusted and have been around for decades).

Second, think about how you can create an emotional attachment to your brand. How people feel about something trumps what they think about it.

Third, decide on a suggestive name or a descriptive name. Suggestive names are more memorable and more defensible. Can your product name suggest the experience people will have from using your product, or can it describe the chief function or benefit of the product?

Fourth, think about how your product creates a distinctive (not necessarily better) experience than that of competitive products. How might your name and reinforce this distinctive experience?

Fifth, think about whether your brand can "own" the terms (or meaning) that are used to search for it? People don't find products by entering a URL in the web address field; they find products by entering a search term. What keywords will customers need to enter to find you on the web or in the app store?

Sixth, decide how best to build trademark rights in your brand and your domain name. Can your logo (visual identity) be clearly expressed as a 16×16 pixel icon in the web address bar? Think about how Facebook (f), Twitter (t), and LinkedIn (in) express their brands with simple, easy-to- identify, letters or symbols.

Things to Do and Avoid

Research what names have become good brands — and why. Understand why some product names failed to resonate with customers.

Write a list of 20 adjectives that customers would use to describe your product.

Write a list of 10 competitor names and order them from favorite to least favorite.

Assemble a group of friends and associates who are also likely users of your product. View the adjectives and competitor names. Brainstorm a list of possible names that (1) evoke the qualities of your product, (2) can be spelled phonetically with less than four syllables and (3) have an appropriate domain name available.

Test the names you like and see if they are available. Checkout NameBoy and Domain Name Generator.

Understand the visual connections your names have by testing them at Visual Thesaurus.

Conduct a Trademark Search to see if others have a similar name or mark.

Before you test the names publicly, register the domain names at GoDaddy or other domain name registrar.

Pitch and test your name at UsabilityHub or MTurk.

Run a mini ad campaign using the names on Google AdWords, Linkedin and/or Facebook to see what kind of draw they have. What are others paying to buy those keywords?

Once you settle on a name, have a graphic designer work on several graphical implementations. Check out UpWork and 99Designs.

Have the graphic designer deliver the logo in black and white, greyscale and color versions, as well as high-resolution and low-resolution formats for each as a EPS vector file and as a PNG file with a transparent background.

Test the comps using the same process as above.

Develop a branding strategy around your name and logo.

Recommended Readings & Resources

[Made to Stick: Why Some Ideas Survive and Others Die](#) Book by Dan and Chip Heath

[Contagious: Why Things Catch On](#) Book by Jonah Berger

[WordLab](#)
Online community dedicated to naming and branding.

[RhymeZone](#)
Rhyming dictionary and thesaurus.

[Igor Naming Guide](#)
Everything you've always wanted to know about naming companies, products and services.

[The Name Inspector](#)
10 company name types on TechCrunch: Pros and cons.

[How to Name Your Startup](#)
by Sam Shank, CEO and Co-Founder at HotelTonight

[Advanced Tips on Naming a Business](#) 5 Tips for Name Storming

Outsource Ancillary Functions

"The important thing about outsourcing or global sourcing is that it becomes a very powerful tool to leverage talent, improve productivity and reduce work cycles."

- Azim Premji, Indian business tycoon and philanthropist

As a startup, just about everything you need to develop your product and launch your company can be outsourced. The rule of thumb is to outsource every function that is not a core competency and not absolutely required to be performed in-house. This includes engineering, manufacturing, testing, packaging, shipping, project management, design, quality assurance, customer service, payment processing, payroll, accounting, legal, marketing, public relations, and hosting. The most cost-effective strategy is to be a virtual company for as long as you can.

One of the biggest mistakes startups make is spending too much money on office space and too much time on general and administrative functions. The most critical function of a startup company is to serve the customer and to continually adjust the product offering as needed to profit from the relationship. Never outsource your company's relationship with the customer. Outsource all the ancillary functions needed to deliver your product to the customer and operate the business.

Things to Think About and Decide

First, think about every mission-critical function that needs to be performed to bring your product to market.

Second, decide which functions (core competencies) should be performed in-house and which functions should be outsourced for the next 12-18 months.

Third, think about who you know that can perform outsourced functions, or who can introduce you to reputable partners and suppliers.

Fourth, think about which suppliers might provide discounts or accept equity or a combination of cash and equity to you as a startup.

Things to Do and Avoid

List the key functions that you will need to launch and operate your offering for 12 months.

Rate each function on a scale of 1 to 10 as to whether it should be outsourced with 1 being "outsourced" and with 10 being "in-house," and also rate the importance of each item to the success of the business with 10 being "most important."

Draft a one to five-page request for proposal ("RFP") to identify vendors for the most important functions that you need to outsource over the next 3-6 months.

Send the RFP to at least three target vendors and post information from the RFP to appropriate online vendor markets and forums.

Negotiate with each appropriate vendor for reduced startup pricing by offering barter, referrals, deferred payment, equity, or any other compensation vehicle.

Set up a vendor review system to regularly measure the results they provided, particularly as it relates to delivering on time, on budget, and according to specification.

Recommended Readings & Resources

[How to Build a Better Business with Outsourcing](#) Entrepreneur Magazine

[Top 10 Tips for Outsourcing Success](#) About.com

[Top 15 Outsource Platforms](#)
Skipzopedia

[Channel Partners and Service Providers](#) Video, Mike ODonnell, StartupBiz

[The Art of Bootstrapping](#)
Guy Kawasaki

[LinkedIn](#)
Search companies and groups for reputable outsource partners.

Draft Guerilla Marketing and Sales Plan

> *"Guerrilla marketing is needed because it gives small businesses a delightfully unfair advantage: certainty in an uncertain world, economy in a high-priced world, simplicity in a complicated world, marketing awareness in a clueless world."*
>
> - Jay Conrad Levinson, Father of Guerrilla Marketing

The specifics of how you will create demand (marketing) and how you will generate revenue (sales) should be detailed in a Go-to-Market Guerilla Marketing and Sales Plan that is separate from the business plan.

Unless you have millions of dollars for advertising and promotion – and to deploy a large direct sales force – you have no choice but to do guerilla marketing. There are many books, blogs, and how-to resources available on the subject. They all boil down to three things:

1. How will you generate *awareness* for your product among the target audience?

2. How will you create customer *affinity* for your product over competing products?

3. How will you facilitate customer *advocacy* of your product that virally creates more customers?

Those are the key marketing objectives of every startup. Sales, on the other hand, comprise a very different set of functions. Sales is a contact sport. It is done with cold calls/emails, one-on-one meetings, networking events and old fashion customer service. Sales *closes* the deal and gets the order. Your marketing and sales plan should distinctly address the strategies, tactics and actions for both marketing and selling your product.

Things to Think About and Decide

First, think about all the ways you could reach your target customers with as little money as possible.

Second, think about the "story" you want to tell them and what form that should take, such as a video, a trial, a sample, or a testimonial from a real customer.

Third, think about who the influencers are in the marketplace. Are there certain people that if they used your product could influence hundreds or thousands of others to buy it?

Fourth, think about which sales channels are best for your product. Will you sell direct? Will you sell through wholesalers, distributors, or retailers?

Fifth, decide on your budget and determine which guerilla marketing strategies and tactics you can afford to do a [soft launch](#) of your product.

Things to Do and Avoid

Estimate your [cost of customer acquisition](#) and the [lifetime value of the average customer](#). Continually measure these metrics until you get accurate and predictable numbers.

Update all of your social media accounts to have a serious profile picture and professional personal description, removing any comments, photos, jokes or other material that may be viewed as unprofessional. Customers and investors "buy" the people behind a startup before they buy the product.

Hire a talented (and experienced) copywriter on contract. It's one of the best marketing investments you can make.

Develop an email mailing list of at least 25 friends, associates, advisers, and target customers that you will send monthly progress updates to about your business and progress. Enroll these people as brand ambassadors.

Write at least 15 phrases for Google, Facebook, LinkedIn, or other high-traffic social media site that your customers use. Create and test different ads that capture your positioning. Refine the ads based on click-thrus.

Test two or three different landing pages for your web site and track views, clicks and conversions.

After you have tested various landing page designs, create and launch a website or blog. Test the site on various services like UsabilityHub.com.

Create company pages on Facebook, Twitter and other social media sites that your customers use. Deploy a system to post content to your blog and social media pages. Track the results.

Identify 6-10 journalists or bloggers that have covered your market and related companies. Add an insightful comment to each relevant story written by each of them and link to the comment from your blog.

Do not hire a PR firm for your launch. Instead, identify three newsworthy milestones that your company has achieved (or will achieve) and have your copywriter draft three press releases. Send out one press release every 3-4 weeks.

Do not hire a Search Engine Optimization (SEO) firm or consultant. You don't have enough money or market awareness (yet) to dominate keywords. Instead, use free tools like Google Analytics and free trial accounts with services like Moz to optimize your website with the appropriate keywords, tags, labels, and metadata.

Recommended Readings & Resources

[Startup Marketing and Sales](#)
Video by Geoff Wilson and Steve Tingiris

[Startup Selling](#)
Video by Mike ODonnell, StartupBiz

[Newsjacking](#)
The art and science of injecting your ideas into a breaking news story and generating media coverage and social media engagement.

[Trust Me, I'm Lying: Confessions of a Media Manipulator](#) Great book by Ryan Holiday

[Strategic Sales Presentations](#) Book by Jack Malcolm

[Fiverr.com](#)
Hire people to answer your questions, perform small tasks.

[MechanticalTurk – Amazon](#)
Conduct market research. Survey your target audience. Mobilize workers to complete small tasks for your startup.

[iStockPhoto](#) and [123RF.com](#)
Royalty free stock photography, images and clip art.

[MailChimp](#)
Build and manage an email list of customers and supporters. Send emails to opt-in list.

[ReTargeter](#) and Google [AdWords](#)
Ad platforms for driving traffic to your website. Create launch ad campaigns with banner ads and pay-per-click text ads.

[tChat](#)
Monitor and chat about a topic; increase your presence on Twitter.

[Webpage Test](#)
Test your website's performance.

[Wufoo Form Builder](#) and [TypeForm](#)
Great app for creating and managing forms on your website or blog.

[Screencast-O-Matic.com](#)
Capture screen shots of your app; record an online demo.

[Skitch](#) and [Snag It](#)
Annotate, edit and share your screen shots with Skitch. Capture screen shots with Snag It. [Tech Smith](#) also offers a video production app, but it is quite pricey for most startups.

Implement a low-cost Customer Relationship Management platform, [like these](#).

Use a [Press Release Distribution Service](#) to distribute worthy product launch news to targeted media outlets.

Capitalize the Company

> *"There's nothing wrong with raising venture capital. Many lean startups are ambitious and are able to deploy large amounts of capital. What differentiates them is their disciplined approach to determining when to spend money: after the fundamental elements of the business model have been empirically validated."*
>
> - Eric Ries, Author, Lean Startup

Novice entrepreneurs spend too much time trying to raise money. It's a very time-consuming process that takes six months if you have a smoking hot business -- and it takes forever if you don't. Seasoned entrepreneurs don't waste time chasing investors until such time that their business can afford them to do it and the odds of success are good.

All you should be thinking about and doing at the start is getting customers; they are the best way to finance your business. If you get traction in the market, you have a better chance of raising money at reasonable terms. The best time to raise money is when you don't need it.

At the outset, you need to be able to capitalize the company with "insider" money. Insider money is invested by the founders and possibly by family members and friends. This is called seed capital. You're going to need enough seed capital to accomplish most of the things outlined in the previous chapters, including forming the company, conducting primary research, building a prototype, scrubbing the plan, and securing the intellectual property.

Outside investors are NOT going to give you money to accomplish these tasks unless you are a Rock Star entrepreneur with a successful track record. Even Mark Zuckerberg and his friends had to finance Facebook with their own money until they were able to show traction. The possible exception is what is called "convertible debt," or a "bridge loan." These financing instruments may be available if you have exceptional intellectual property (like a patent) or are using the money to purchase tangible assets.

If things go well, you're probably going to need outside capital at some point. Outside capital means money from accredited investors. It may be grants or loans. The SBA is a good lending source. There are also a bunch of asset-based lenders, including PayPal and Guidant.

For some startups, equity capital is available from angel investors or venture capitalists, meaning you will need to sell shares in your company. This is usually done as a Series A Financing.

The act of taking outside money increases a company's legal obligations and liabilities significantly. The process of investor due diligence is akin to undergoing an intense tax audit. Everything there is to know about you and your company will be discovered and scrutinized.

Things to Think About and Decide

First, think about how much money you will need to accomplish the steps outlined in this guide, to get the business to a point where it is either cash-flow positive or able to attract outside capital.

Second, think about how long it will take to accomplish the steps and how long you can go without a salary.

Third, decide how much of your personal savings or your credit you and your co-founders can afford to risk.

Fourth, think about how much seed capital you might be able to raise from family and friends to cover the shortfall between what you need and what you and your team can invest.

Fifth, think about what other sources of capital may be available to you, such as loans or grants.

Sixth, decide whether your business is fundable and what needs to happen to attract funding.

Things to Do and Avoid

Do not pitch investors until you are 100% ready with a launched offering, some market traction, and prepared materials.

When you are ready to raise money, identify three to five critical growth metrics that will validate your revenue assumptions with investors.

Calculate the amount of money you need to raise to operate for a full year multiplied by 1.5.

Develop a use of proceeds for the desired money by identifying at least three quantifiable business objectives related to revenue that you can realistically achieve within three months, such as a specific number of customers or a volume of usage.

Update your Executive Summary and PowerPoint presentations with the amount of money and the use of proceeds.

Identify at least 50 local angels, angel groups, early-stage venture capitalists and other investors in a spreadsheet with their name, email address, telephone number, title, company, relationship, LinkedIn (or similar profile), related investments and notes.

Identify at least three events over the next month where you can meet investors from your target list face-to-face and make plans to attend the event. BONUS: apply to present at pitch events.

Create an investor pitch deck that shows how you are mitigating the risk for investors and offering the potential of a substantial return on investment.

Create a detailed company profile on AngelList, GUST, and/or another startup company network.

Check out the appropriate Crowdfunding platforms for your space.

List your founders and your company in CrunchBase.

Create, test, and refine a 30 second "elevator pitch" on your company. A sixth grader should understand it.

Assemble all the due diligence documents that will be required by prospective investors.

Recommended Readings & Resources

Raising Venture Capital, Pitching to Investors Travis Milks, Stonehenge Capital

The 10/20/30 Rule of PowerPoint Guy Kawasaki

10 Dumb Things Entrepreneurs Say to Investors by Mike ODonnell

Top 10 Toughest Questions Asked of Startup Founders (and how to answer them): PART 1 by Mike ODonnell

Top 10 Toughest Questions Asked of Startup Founders (and how to answer them): PART 2 by Mike ODonnell

Tough Questions Smart Startup Founders Should Ask Prospective Investors by Mike ODonnell

Startups.com
Startup and funding resources.

AngelList
List your startup, network with angel investors. A good place to see what other startups are in your space, going after the same market.

[When Your Startup is Fundable but You Aren't](#)
by Mike ODonnell

[Gust](#)
Gust connects startups with the largest collection of investors across the world.

[KickStarter](#)
Raise money for creative projects or to develop your app.

[Florida Funders](#)
A crowdfunding portal that connects accredited investors with startups seeking funding.

[Due Diligence Checklist](#) and [Sample Term Sheet,](#) StartupBiz.com

[SAFE Note](#) and [Convertible Note](#) docs, by Cooley

[Crowdfunding Platforms](#), by Fundly

[The Five Star Startup:](#) A Guide for Determining Which Startup Opportunities are Worth Your Time and Money, by Mike ODonnell.

Operate the Company

"There's no such thing as work-life balance. There are work-life choices, and you make them, and they have consequences."

-Jack Welch, CEO, General Electric

The hardest part about starting a company is running it effectively. Companies don't run themselves. That may sound trite and obvious, but unless you devise a system for running your company, it will consume you and take you away from focusing on the reason it exists to begin with – providing a great product and getting and keeping customers.

Entrepreneurs create, refine, and manage ideas. Big corporations create, refine, and manage process. To grow your company – to make it successful – you must put in place good systems and processes. The good news is that the availability of tools necessary to create good processes is plentiful and the costs are inexpensive for most startups.

Things to Think About and Decide

First, think about how you will list and prioritize the most important things that must get done each week, to move your company to the next step.

Second, decide how you and your team will communicate and collaborate with each other.

Third, think carefully about which company functions you should delegate or outsource, and which functions you or your co-founder(s) should manage.

Fourth, think about how to leverage the talent, information, space, supplies, equipment, tools, and other resources of your connections (family, friends, partners, suppliers, customers) to help run your company.

Things to Do and Avoid

Do not reinvent the wheel and try to build or customize systems and processes, at least at the start. There is a tool, template, or service for just about everything your company needs to operate.

Standardize on an email and web service and install it on all your devices.

Standardize on a phone and video conferencing service that your team will use to communicate with each other and with customers and partners, such as Skype, Google Meet, Go-to-Meeting, ZOOM, or Webex.

Standardize on a document suite such as GoogleDocs or Microsoft Office.

Standardize on a good project management tool.

Get in the habit of writing a company update at least once per month and share it with your team, shareholders, and influencers.

Develop a dashboard or score card (Key Performance Metrics – KPI's) of all key business metrics and share them with everyone weekly.

Meet regularly with your team and advisors and focus on key milestones.

Recommended Readings & Resources

[The E-Myth: Why Most Small Businesses Don't Work and What to Do About It](#)
A classic, simply the best book you will ever read on running a

successful company.

[SCORE, Starting a Business Library](#)
Loads of great resources for starting and operating a small business.

[Google WorkSpace](#)
Online office suite including word processing, spreadsheets, e-mail, and calendar.

[ZOHO](#)
The operating system for any small business.

[FreshBooks](#)
Online invoicing, accounting and billing software.

[Reputation.com](#)
Monitor your reputation and those of your company and products.

[Getting Things Done](#)
by David Allen – Tactics to organize efficient task lists.

[The Process of Creating Good Processes in a Startup](#) ([Part 1](#)) and ([Part 2](#)).

[StartupBiz.com](#)
Legal and business templates for startup companies.

[Trello](#)
Manage all your ideas and due dates and keep track of what you're in the process of completing.

[Asana](#)
Teamwork without email.

[FaxZero](#)
Send and receive faxes through your email.

[RescueTime](#)
Monitor how you spend your time on your computer and mobile devices.

[Remember the Milk](#)
A to-do list manager that you can sync with all your devices, share tasks with others, and get email or text reminders of things you need to get done.

[Evernote](#)
Remember everything using text, photo or audio notes, and clippings of websites.

[Feedly](#)
One of the best RSS readers on the market, a place to keep up with all the latest from your favorite blogs and publications.

[TaskRabbit](#)
Outsource any task you really don't want to do, from running errands to planning the details of your next event.

[IFTTT](#)
"If This Then That," helps different apps, online programs, and services work together to make your life easier.

[Lifehacker](#)
Solutions to problems you didn't even know you had, from how to handle IT glitches to productivity tips.

[Eventbrite](#)
Great tool for finding events and for planning and promoting your own events.

Conference Bites
An aggregation of all the notes you missed at various industry conferences.

Udemy
A mix of free and paid online classes with a solid rating system.

Upworthy
Social issues that matter most, with viral videos and images to stimulate ideas for your products and services.

TED
Unlimited inspiration and cool people doing amazing things.

Quora
Ask questions, get answers. Good place to crowdsource things you want to know.

99U
Strategies for turning your ideas into action.

Visual.ly
Create your own infographic on your market or product.

Behance
Showcase your design work, get ideas from really talented people.

Bubbl.us
Gather your thoughts, save them for later to continue the thought process, or print or email them to yourself.

PayScale
Best source of data to find out what positions pay in different geographical areas. Use it before offering someone a raise (or asking for one).

DiSC for Entrepreneurs and Startup Teams
Time-tested assessments and personalized reports to help surface entrepreneurial and team leadership and workstyles, and behavioral predispositions.

Mint
Link your credit cards, bank accounts, and loans to have a total online system that tracks your spending, saving, and financial health.

Fast Company
One of the best weekly reads on business news.

Mashable
The "leading source for news, information, and resources for the Connected Generation," Mashable reports on our digital lives.

Inc.
Good read for productivity tips, management advice, and secrets of some of the world's most successful people.

Harvard Business Review
Tips on everything from corporate strategy to managing people.

Bloomberg BusinessWeek
Smart, in-depth reporting about the biggest business, financial, and stock market issues.

First Round Review
One of the best collections of content for startups. Subscribe to their newsletter for in-depth articles on all topics related to building a successful business.

theSkimm
Get the day's top headlines in one newsletter, makes staying current easy.

Bonus Templates

These templates are provided as samples and not intended for use without the advice and counsel of licensed professionals.

More templates are available for free download at https://www.startupbiz.com/templates/.

Articles of Incorporation
[Name of Company Here]

The undersigned, for the purposes of incorporating and organizing a corporation under the General Corporation Law of the State of [State of Incorporation Here], does hereby certify as follows:

ARTICLE I - NAME
The name of the Corporation is [state name here].

ARTICLE II - REGISTERED AGENT
The name of its registered agent and the address of its registered office in the state of [state] is:

Registered Agent	Registered Office
[Name]	[Address, County]

ARTICLE III - PURPOSE

The purpose of the Corporation is to engage in any lawful act or activity for which corporations may be organized under the General Corporation Law of the state of [Name of State Here].

ARTICLE IV - SHARES

The total number of shares of stock which the Corporation shall have authority to issue is [spell out number] [(number of shares)] shares of common stock, par value [value of shares, i.e., $.01] per share.

ARTCILE V - INCORPORATOR

The name and mailing address of the incorporator of the Corporation is:

[Name of Officer or Attorney for the Company]

ARTICLE VI - INITIAL DIRECTORS

The powers of the incorporator are to terminate upon the filing of this Certificate of Incorporation. The initial board of directors shall consist of one (1) director who shall serve until the first annual meeting of stockholders and the election and qualification of the successors. The name and address of the person who shall serve as the initial director is: [Name and address of initial director for the company]

Except with respect to the initial board of directors, the number of directors constituting the board of directors shall be determined in the manner specified in the Bylaws. In the absence of such a provision in the Bylaws, the board shall consist of the number of directors constituting the initial board of directors.

ARTICLE VII - BOARD OF DIRECTORS

In furtherance and not in limitation of the powers conferred by the laws of the State of [state], the Board of Directors is expressly authorized and empowered to make, alter and repeal the Bylaws of the Corporation, subject to the power of the stockholders of the Corporation to alter or repeal and bylaw made by the Board of Directors. Elections of directors need not be by written ballot unless the Bylaws of the Corporation shall so provide.

ARTCILE VIII - LIMITATION ON DIRECTOR LIABILITY

A director of the Corporation shall not be personally liable to the Corporation or its stockholders for monetary damages for conduct as a director or for breach of fiduciary duty as a director, except to the extent such exemption from liability or limitation thereof is not permitted under the General Corporation Law of the State of [state] as the same exists or may hereafter be amended. Any amendment, repeal or modification of the foregoing sentence shall not adversely affect any right or protection of a director of the Corporation existing hereunder with respect to any act or omission occurring prior to such amendment, repeal or modification.

ARTICLE IX - AMENDMENTS

The Corporation reserves the right at any time, and from time to time, to amend, alter, change or repeal any provision contained in this Certificate of Incorporation, and other provisions authorized by the laws of the State of [state] at the time in force may be added or inserted, in the manner now or hereafter prescribed by statue, and all rights, preferences and privileges of whatsoever nature conferred upon the stockholders, directors or any other persons whomsoever by and pursuant to this Certificate of Incorporation in its present form or as hereafter amended are granted subject to the rights reserved in this Article IX.

ARTICLE X – PREEMPTIVE RIGHTS

The stockholders of this Corporation have no preemptive rights to acquire additional shares of this Corporation.

ARTICLE XI - CUMULATIVE VOTING

Stockholders entitled to vote at any election of directors are entitled to cumulate votes by multiplying the number of votes they are entitled to cast by the number of directors for whom they are entitled to vote and to cast the product for a single candidate or distribute the product among two or more candidates.

IN WITNESS WHEREOF, the undersigned, being the sole incorporator hereinabove named, for the purpose of forming a corporation pursuant to the General Corporation Law of the State of [state], does make this Certificate, hereby declaring and certifying that this is his/her act and deed and the facts herein stated are true, and, accordingly, have hereunto set his/her hand this [date] day of [month], [year].

[Signature]   [Print Name]
Incorporator

Company By-laws

OF

[Company Name]

ARTICLE I

Stockholders

Section I.1.<u>Annual Meetings</u>. An annual meeting of stockholders shall be held for the election of directors at such date, time and place, either within or without the State of [state of incorporation], as may be designated by resolution of the Board of Directors from time to time. Any other proper business may be transacted at the annual meeting.

Section I.2.<u>Special Meetings</u>. Special meetings of stockholders for any purpose or purposes may be called at any time by the Board of Directors, or by a committee of the Board of Directors that has been duly designated by the Board of Directors and whose powers and authority, as expressly provided in a resolution of the Board of Directors, include the power to call such meetings, but such special meetings may not be called by any other person or persons.

Section I.3.<u>Notice of Meetings</u>. Whenever stockholders are required or permitted to take any action at a meeting, a written notice of the meeting shall be given that shall state the place, date and hour of the meeting and, in the case of a special meeting, the purpose or purposes for which the meeting is called. Unless otherwise provided by law, the certificate of incorporation or these bylaws, the written notice of any meeting shall be given not less than ten nor more than sixty days before the date of the meeting to each stockholder entitled to vote at such meeting. If mailed, such notice shall be deemed to be given when deposited in the United States mail, postage prepaid, directed to the stockholder at his address as it appears on the records of the corporation.

Section I.4.<u>Adjournments</u>. Any meeting of stockholders, annual or special, may adjourn from time to time to reconvene at the same or some other place, and notice need not be given of any such adjourned meeting if the time and place thereof are announced at the meeting at which the adjournment is taken. At the adjourned meeting the corporation may transact any business which might have been transacted at the original meeting. If the adjournment is for more than thirty days, or if after the adjournment a new record date is fixed for the adjourned meeting, notice of the adjourned meeting shall be given to each stockholder of record entitled to vote at the meeting.

Section I.5.<u>Quorum</u>. Except as otherwise provided by law, the certificate of incorporation or these bylaws, at each meeting of stockholders the presence in person or by proxy of the holders of a majority in voting power of the outstanding shares of stock entitled to vote at the meeting shall be necessary and sufficient to constitute a quorum. In the absence of a quorum, the stockholders so present may, by majority vote, adjourn the meeting from time to time in the manner provided in Section 1.4 of these bylaws until a quorum shall attend. Shares of its own stock belonging to the corporation or to another corporation, if a majority of the shares entitled to vote in the election of directors of such other corporation is held, directly or indirectly, by the corporation, shall neither be entitled to vote nor be counted for quorum purposes; provided, however, that the foregoing shall not limit the right of the corporation or any subsidiary of the corporation to vote stock, including but not limited to its own stock, held by it in a fiduciary capacity.

Section I.6.<u>Organization</u>. Meetings of stockholders shall be presided over by the Chairman of the Board, if any, or in his absence by the Vice Chairman of the Board, if any, or in his absence by the President, or in his absence by a Vice President, or in the absence of the foregoing persons by a chairman designated by the Board of Directors, or in the absence of such designation by a chairman chosen at the meeting. The Secretary shall act as secretary of the meeting, but in his absence the chairman of the meeting may appoint any person to act as secretary of the meeting. The chairman of the meeting shall announce at the meeting of stockholders the date and time of the opening and the closing of the polls for each matter upon which the stockholders will vote.

Section I.7.<u>Voting; Proxies</u>. Except as otherwise provided by the certificate of incorporation, each stockholder entitled to vote at any meeting of stockholders shall be entitled to one vote for each share of stock held by him which has voting power upon the matter in question. Each stockholder entitled to vote at a meeting of stockholders or to express consent or dissent to corporate action in writing without a meeting may authorize another person or persons to act for him by proxy, but no such proxy shall be voted or acted upon after three years from its date, unless the proxy provides for a longer period. A proxy shall be irrevocable if it states that it is irrevocable and if, and only as long as, it is coupled with an interest sufficient in law to support an irrevocable power. A stockholder may revoke any proxy which is not irrevocable by attending the meeting and voting in person or by filing an instrument in writing revoking the proxy or by delivering a proxy in accordance with applicable law bearing a later date to the Secretary of the corporation. Voting at meetings of stockholders need not be by written ballot. At all meetings of stockholders for the election of directors a plurality of the votes cast shall be sufficient to elect. All other elections and questions shall, unless otherwise provided by law, the certificate of incorporation or these bylaws, be decided by the affirmative vote of the holders of a majority in voting power of the shares of stock which are present in person or by proxy and entitled to vote thereon.

Section I.8.<u>Fixing Date for Determination of Stockholders of Record</u>. In order that the corporation may determine the stockholders entitled to notice of or to vote at any meeting of stockholders or any adjournment thereof, or to express consent to corporate action in writing without a meeting, or entitled to receive payment of any dividend or other distribution or allotment of any rights, or entitled to exercise any rights in respect of any change, conversion or exchange of stock or for the purpose of any other lawful action, the Board of Directors may fix a record date, which record date shall not precede the date upon which the resolution fixing the record date is adopted by the Board of Directors, and which record date: (1) in the case of determination of stockholders entitled to vote at any meeting of stockholders or adjournment thereof, shall, unless otherwise required by law, not be more than sixty nor less than ten days before the date of such meeting; (2) in the case of determination of stockholders entitled to express consent to corporate action in writing without a meeting, shall not be more than ten days from the date upon which the resolution fixing the record date is adopted by the Board of Directors; and (3) in the case of any other action, shall not be more than sixty days prior to such other action. If no record date is fixed: (1) the record date for determining stockholders entitled to notice of or to vote at a meeting of stockholders shall be at the close of business on the day next preceding the day on which notice is given, or, if notice is waived, at the close of business on the day next preceding the day on which the meeting is held; (2) the record date for determining stockholders entitled to express consent to corporate action in writing without a meeting, when no prior action of the Board of Directors is required by law, shall be the first date on which a signed written consent setting forth the action taken or proposed to be taken is delivered to the corporation in accordance with applicable law, or, if prior action by the Board of Directors is required by law, shall be at the close of business on the day on which the Board of Directors adopts the resolution taking such prior action; and (3) the record date for determining stockholders for any other purpose shall be at the close of business on the day on which the Board of Directors adopts the resolution relating thereto. A determination of stockholders of record entitled to notice of or to vote at a meeting of stockholders shall apply to any adjournment of the meeting; provided, however, that the Board of Directors may fix a new record date for the adjourned meeting.

Section I.9. <u>List of Stockholders Entitled to Vote</u>. The Secretary shall prepare and make, at least ten days before every meeting of stockholders, a complete list of the stockholders entitled to vote at the meeting, arranged in alphabetical order, and showing the address of each stockholder and the number of shares registered in the name of each stockholder. Such list shall be open to the examination of any stockholder, for any purpose germane to the meeting, during ordinary business hours, for a period of at least ten days prior to the meeting, either at a place within the city where the meeting is to be held, which place shall be specified in the notice of the meeting, or if not so specified, at the place where the meeting is to be held. The list shall also be produced and kept at the time and place of the meeting during the whole time thereof and may be inspected by any stockholder who is present. Upon the willful neglect or refusal of the directors to produce such a list at any meeting for the election of directors, they shall be ineligible for election to any office at such meeting. Except as otherwise provided by law, the stock ledger shall be the only evidence as to who are the stockholders entitled to examine the stock ledger, the list of stockholders or the books of the corporation, or to vote in person or by proxy at any meeting of stockholders.

Section I.10. <u>Action By Consent of Stockholders</u>. Unless otherwise restricted by the certificate of incorporation, any action required or permitted to be taken at any annual or special meeting of the stockholders may be taken without a meeting, without prior notice and without a vote, if a consent or consents in writing, setting forth the action so taken, shall be signed by the holders of outstanding stock having not less than the minimum number of votes that would be necessary to authorize or take such action at a meeting at which all shares entitled to vote thereon were present and voted and shall be delivered (by hand or by certified or registered mail, return receipt requested) to the corporation by delivery to its registered office in the State of [state of incorporation], its principal place of business, or an officer or agent of the corporation having custody of the book in which proceedings of minutes of stockholders are recorded. Prompt notice of the taking of the corporate action without a meeting by less than unanimous written consent shall be given to those stockholders who have not consented in writing.

Section I.11. <u>Inspectors of Election</u>. The corporation may, and shall if required by law, in advance of any meeting of stockholders, appoint one or more inspectors of election, who may be employees of the corporation, to act at the meeting or any adjournment thereof and to make a written report thereof. The corporation may designate one or more persons as alternate inspectors to replace any inspector who fails to act. In the event that no inspector so appointed or designated is able to act at a meeting of stockholders, the person presiding at the meeting shall appoint one or more inspectors to act at the meeting. Each inspector, before entering upon the discharge of his or her duties, shall take and sign an oath to execute faithfully the duties of inspector with strict impartiality and according to the best of his or her ability. The inspector or inspectors so appointed or designated shall (i) ascertain the number of shares of capital stock of the corporation outstanding and the voting power of each such share, (ii) determine the shares of capital stock of the corporation represented at the meeting and the validity of proxies and ballots, (iii) count all votes and ballots, (iv) determine and retain for a reasonable period a record of the disposition of any challenges made to any determination by the inspectors, and (v) certify their determination of the number of shares of capital stock of the corporation represented at the meeting and such inspectors' count of all votes and ballots. Such certification and report shall specify such other information as may be required by law. In determining the validity and counting of proxies and ballots cast at any meeting of stockholders of the corporation, the inspectors may consider such information as is permitted by applicable law. No person who is a candidate for an office at an election may serve as an inspector at such election.

Section I.12. <u>Conduct of Meetings</u>. The Board of Directors of the corporation may adopt by resolution such rules and regulations for the conduct of the meeting of stockholders as it shall deem appropriate. Except to the extent inconsistent with such rules and regulations as adopted by the Board of Directors, the chairman of any meeting of stockholders shall have the right and authority to prescribe such rules, regulations and procedures and to do all such acts as, in the judgment of such chairman, are appropriate for the proper conduct of the meeting. Such rules, regulations or procedures, whether adopted by the Board of Directors or prescribed by the chairman of the meeting, may include, without limitation, the following: (i) the establishment of an agenda or order of business for the meeting; (ii) rules and procedures for maintaining order at the meeting and the safety of those present; (iii) limitations on attendance at or participation in the meeting to stockholders of record of the corporation, their duly authorized and constituted proxies or such other persons as the chairman of the meeting shall determine; (iv) restrictions on entry to the meeting after the time fixed for the commencement thereof; and (v) limitations on the time allotted to questions or comments by participants. Unless and to the extent determined by the Board of Directors or the chairman of the meeting, meetings of stockholders shall not be required to be held in accordance with the rules of parliamentary procedure.

ARTICLE II

Board of Directors

Section II.1. <u>Number; Qualifications</u>. The Board of Directors shall consist of one or more members, the number thereof to be determined from time to time by resolution of the Board of Directors. Directors need not be stockholders.

Section II.2. <u>Election; Resignation; Removal; Vacancies</u>. The Board of Directors shall initially consist of the persons named as directors in the certificate of incorporation, and each director so elected shall hold office until the first annual meeting of stockholders or until his successor is elected and qualified. At the first annual meeting of stockholders and at each annual meeting thereafter, the stockholders shall elect directors each of whom shall hold office for a term of one year or until his successor is elected and qualified. Any director may resign at any time upon written notice to the corporation. Any newly created directorship or any vacancy occurring in the Board of Directors for any cause may be filled by a majority of the remaining members of the Board of Directors, although such majority is less than a quorum, or by a plurality of the votes cast at a meeting of stockholders, and each director so elected shall hold office until the expiration of the term of office of the director whom he has replaced or until his successor is elected and qualified.

Section II.3. Regular Meetings. Regular meetings of the Board of Directors may be held at such places within or without the State of [state of incorporation] and at such times as the Board of Directors may from time to time determine, and if so determined notices thereof need not be given.

Section II.4. Special Meetings. Special meetings of the Board of Directors may be held at any time or place within or without the State of [state of incorporation] whenever called by the President, any Vice President, the Secretary, or by any member of the Board of Directors. Notice of a special meeting of the Board of Directors shall be given by the person or persons calling the meeting at least twenty-four hours before the special meeting.

Section II.5. Telephonic Meetings Permitted. Members of the Board of Directors, or any committee designated by the Board of Directors, may participate in a meeting thereof by means of conference telephone or similar communications equipment by means of which all persons participating in the meeting can hear each other, and participation in a meeting pursuant to this bylaw shall constitute presence in person at such meeting.

Section II.6. Quorum; Vote Required for Action. At all meetings of the Board of Directors a majority of the whole Board of Directors shall constitute a quorum for the transaction of business. Except in cases in which the certificate of incorporation, these bylaws or applicable law otherwise provides, the vote of a majority of the directors present at a meeting at which a quorum is present shall be the act of the Board of Directors.

Section II.7. Organization. Meetings of the Board of Directors shall be presided over by the Chairman of the Board, if any, or in his absence by the Vice Chairman of the Board, if any, or in his absence by the President, or in their absence by a chairman chosen at the meeting. The Secretary shall act as secretary of the meeting, but in his absence the chairman of the meeting may appoint any person to act as secretary of the meeting.

Section II.8. Informal Action by Directors. Unless otherwise restricted by the certificate of incorporation or these bylaws, any action required or permitted to be taken at any meeting of the Board of Directors, or of any committee thereof, may be taken without a meeting if all members of the Board of Directors or such committee, as the case may be, consent thereto in writing, and the writing or writings are filed with the minutes of proceedings of the Board of Directors or such committee.

ARTICLE III

Committees

Section III.1. <u>Committees</u>. The Board of Directors may, by resolution passed by a majority of the whole Board of Directors, designate one or more committees, each committee to consist of one or more of the directors of the corporation. The Board of Directors may designate one or more directors as alternate members of any committee, who may replace any absent or disqualified member at any meeting of the committee. In the absence of disqualification of a member of the committee, the member or members thereof present at any meeting and not disqualified from voting, whether or not he or they constitute a quorum, may unanimously appoint another member of the Board of Directors to act at the meeting in place of any such absent or disqualified member. Any such committee, to the extent permitted by law and to the extent provided in the resolution of the Board of Directors, shall have and may exercise all the powers and authority of the Board of Directors in the management of the business and affairs of the corporation, and may authorize the seal of the corporation to be affixed to all papers which may require it.

Section III.2. <u>Committee Rules</u>. Unless the Board of Directors otherwise provides, each committee designated by the Board of Directors may make, alter and repeal rules for the conduct of its business. In the absence of such rules each committee shall conduct its business in the same manner as the Board of Directors conducts its business pursuant to Article II of these bylaws.

ARTICLE IV

<u>Officers</u>

Section IV.1. <u>Executive Officers; Election; Qualifications; Term of Office; Resignation: Removal; Vacancies</u>. The Board of Directors shall elect from its members a Chairman of the Board and a Vice Chairman of the Board. The Board of Directors shall elect a President and Secretary. The Board of Directors may also choose one or more Vice Presidents, one or more Assistant Secretaries, a Treasurer and one or more Assistant Treasurers. Each such officer shall hold office until the first meeting of the Board of Directors after the annual meeting of stockholders next succeeding his election, and until his successor is elected and qualified or until his earlier resignation or removal. Any officer may resign at any time upon written notice to the corporation. The Board of Directors may remove any officer with or without cause at any time, but such removal shall be without prejudice to the contractual rights of such officer, if any, with the corporation. Any number of offices may be held by the same person. Any vacancy occurring in any office of the corporation by death, resignation, removal or otherwise may be filled for the unexpired portion of the term by the Board of Directors at any regular or special meeting.

Section IV.2. <u>Powers and Duties of Executive Officers</u>. (i) The officers of the corporation shall have such powers and duties in the management of the corporation as may be prescribed in a resolution by the Board of Directors and, to the extent not so provided, as generally pertain to their respective offices, subject to the control of the Board of Directors. The Board of Directors may require any officer, agent or employee to give security for the faithful performance of his duties. (ii) Notwithstanding the foregoing, (a) the Chairman of the Board shall preside at meetings of stockholders and at meetings of the Board of Directors, and, in his absence, the Vice Chairman of the Board shall preside; and (b) the Chairman of the Board and the Vice

Chairman of the Board shall perform such other duties as the Board of Directors shall from time to time determine.

ARTICLE V

Stock

Section V.1. Certificate s. Every holder of stock shall be entitled to have a certificate signed by or in the name of the corporation by the Chairman or Vice Chairman of the

Board of Directors, if any, or the President or a Vice President, and by the Treasurer or an Assistant Treasurer, or the Secretary or an Assistant Secretary, of the corporation certifying the number of shares owned by him in the corporation. Any of or all the signatures on the certificate may be a facsimile. In case any officer, transfer agent or registrar who has signed or whose facsimile signature has been placed upon a certificate shall have ceased to be such officer, transfer agent, or registrar before such certificate is issued, it may be issued by the corporation with the same effect as if he were such officer, transfer agent, or registrar at the date of issue.

Section V.2. Lost, Stolen or Destroyed Stock Certificates; Issuance of New Certificates. The corporation may issue a new certificate of stock in the place of any certificate theretofore issued by it, alleged to have been lost, stolen or destroyed, and the corporation may require the owner of the lost, stolen or destroyed certificate, or his legal representative, to give the corporation a bond sufficient to indemnify it against any claim that may be made against it on account of the alleged loss, theft or destruction of any such certificate or the issuance of such new certificate.

ARTICLE VI

Indemnification

Section VI.1. Right to Indemnification. The corporation shall indemnify and hold harmless, to the fullest extent permitted by applicable law as it presently exists or may hereafter be amended, any person who was or is made or is threatened to be made a party or is otherwise involved in any action, suit or proceeding, whether civil, criminal, administrative or investigative (a "proceeding"), by reason of the fact that he, or a person for whom he is the legal representative, is or was a director or officer of the corporation or is or was serving at the request of the corporation as a director, officer, employee or agent of another corporation or of a partnership, joint venture, trust, enterprise or nonprofit entity, including service with respect to employee benefit plans (an "indemnitee"), against all liability and loss suffered and expenses (including attorneys' fees) reasonably incurred by such indemnitee. The corporation shall be required to indemnify an indemnitee in connection with a proceeding (or part thereof) initiated by such indemnitee only if the initiation of such proceeding (or part thereof) by the indemnitee was authorized by the Board of Directors of the corporation.

Section VI.2. Prepayment of Expenses. The corporation shall pay the expenses (including attorneys' fees) incurred by an indemnitee in defending any proceeding in advance of its final disposition, provided, however, that the payment of expenses incurred by a director or officer in advance of the final disposition of the proceeding shall be made only upon receipt of an undertaking by the director or officer to repay all amounts advanced if it should be ultimately determined that the director or officer is not entitled to be indemnified under this Article or otherwise.

Section VI.3. <u>Claims</u>. If a claim for indemnification or payment of expenses under this Article is not paid in full within sixty days after a written claim therefor by the indemnitee has been received by the corporation, the indemnitee may file suit to recover the unpaid amount of such claim and, if successful in whole or in part, shall be entitled to be paid the expense of prosecuting such claim. In any such action the corporation shall have the burden of proving that the indemnitee was not entitled to the requested indemnification or payment of expenses under applicable law.

Section VI.4. <u>Nonexclusivity of Rights</u>. The rights conferred on any person by this Article VI shall not be exclusive of any other rights which such person may have or hereafter acquire under any statute, provision of the certificate of incorporation, these bylaws, agreement, vote of stockholders or disinterested directors or otherwise.

Section VI.5. <u>Other Indemnification</u>. The corporation's obligation, if any, to indemnify, or advance expenses to, any person who was or is serving at its request as a director, officer, employee or agent of another corporation, partnership, joint venture, trust, enterprise or nonprofit entity shall be reduced by any amount such person may collect as indemnification, or advancement of expenses, from such other corporation, partnership, joint venture, trust, enterprise or nonprofit enterprise.

Section VI.6. <u>Amendment or Repeal</u>. Any repeal or modification of the foregoing provisions of this Article VI shall not adversely affect any right or protection hereunder of any person in respect of any act or omission occurring prior to the time of such repeal or modification.

Section VI.7. <u>Other Capacities</u>. Notwithstanding anything in this Article VI to the contrary, the corporation shall not have any obligation hereunder to indemnify or advance expenses to any person arising out of or in connection with actions taken by such person in his individual capacity and not on behalf of or at the request of the corporation.

ARTICLE VII

<u>Miscellaneous</u>

Section VII.1. <u>Fiscal Year</u>. The fiscal year of the corporation shall be determined by resolution of the Board of Directors.

Section VII.2. <u>Seal</u>. The corporate seal shall have the name of the corporation inscribed thereon and shall be in such form as may be approved from time to time by the Board of Directors.

Section VII.3. <u>Waiver of Notice of Meetings of Stockholders, Directors and Committees</u>. Any written waiver of notice, signed by the person entitled to notice, whether before or after the time stated therein, shall be deemed equivalent to notice. Attendance of a person at a meeting shall constitute a waiver of notice of such meeting, except when the person attends a meeting for the express purpose of objecting, at the beginning of the meeting, to the transaction of any business because the meeting is not lawfully called or convened. Neither the business to be transacted at nor the purpose of any regular or special meeting of the stockholders, directors, or members of a committee of directors need be specified in any written waiver of notice.

Section VII.4. <u>Interested Directors; Quorum</u>. No contract or transaction between the corporation and one or more of its directors or officers, or between the corporation and any other corporation, partnership, association, or other organization in which one or more of its directors or officers are directors or officers, or have a financial interest, shall be void or voidable solely for this reason, or solely because the director or officer is present at or participates in the meeting of the Board of Directors or committee thereof which authorizes the contract or transaction, or solely because his or their votes are counted for such purpose, if: (1) the material facts as to his relationship or interest and as to the contract or transaction are disclosed or are known to the Board of Directors or the committee, and the Board of Directors or committee in good faith authorizes the contract or transaction by the affirmative votes of a majority of the disinterested directors, even though the disinterested directors be less than a quorum; or (2) the material facts as to his relationship or interest and as to the contract or transaction are disclosed or are known to the stockholders entitled to vote thereon, and the contract or transaction is specifically approved in good faith by vote of the stockholders; or (3) the contract or transaction is fair as to the corporation as of the time it is authorized, approved or ratified, by the Board of Directors, a committee thereof, or the stockholders. Common or interested directors may be counted in determining the presence of a quorum at a meeting of the Board of Directors or of a committee which authorizes the contract or transaction.

Section VII.5. <u>Form of Records</u>. Any records maintained by the corporation in the regular course of its business, including its stock ledger, books of account, and minute books, may be kept on, or be in the form of, punch cards, magnetic tape, photographs, microphotographs, or any other information storage device, provided that the records so kept can be converted into clearly legible form within a reasonable time.

Section VII.6. <u>Amendment of Bylaws</u>. These bylaws may be altered or repealed, and new bylaws made, by the Board of Directors, but the stockholders may make additional bylaws and may alter and repeal any bylaws whether adopted by them or otherwise.

Section VII.7. <u>Conflicts</u>. Unless prohibited by law, the contractual or other binding relinquishment or restriction of any privilege or right granted in the certificate of incorporation or
herein, including specifically but without limitation the right of indemnification, by voluntary act of any person otherwise entitled to such privilege or right shall be interpreted to give effect to such relinquishment or restriction.

The undersigned, being the Secretary of the corporation, hereby certifies that these bylaws are the bylaws of [company name] Inc., adopted by consent in lieu of organizational meeting of directors dated as of [date].

DATED as of this [day] day of [month], **20**[year].
Secretary _____

Limited Liability Company (LLC) Partnership Agreement

[company name here]

This Agreement is made and entered into as of the ____ day of _____, 202_ by and between [list partners here] "Members"). The Members desire to form a limited liability company under the laws of the state of [list state the partnership will do business in here] upon the terms and conditions set forth herein.

The parties agree as follows:

1. Definitions -- The following terms used in the Agreement shall have the meanings specified below:

    1. "Act" means the [state] Limited Liability Company Act, as amended from time to time.

    2. "Agreement" means this Agreement of the [company name], LLC as it may be amended from time to time.

    3. "Assignee" means a person who has acquired a Member's Interest in whole or part and has not become a Substitute Member.

    4. "Capital Account" means the account maintained for each Member in accordance with Section 6.5. In the case of a transfer of an interest, the transferee shall succeed to the Capital Account of the transferor or, in the case of a partial transfer, a proportionate share thereof.

    5. "Capital Contribution" means the total amount of money and the fair market value of all property contributed to the Company by each Member pursuant to the terms of the Agreement. Capital Contribution shall also include any amounts paid directly by a Member to any creditor of the Company in respect of any guarantee or similar obligation undertaken by such Member in connection with the Company's operations. Any reference to the Capital Contribution of a Member shall include the Capital Contribution made by a predecessor holder of the interest of such Member.

    6. "Cash Available for Distribution" means all cash receipts of the Company, excluding cash available upon liquidation of the Company, in excess of amounts reasonably required for payment of operating expenses, repayment of current liabilities, repayment of such amounts of Company indebtedness as the Members shall determine necessary or advisable, and the establishment of and additions to such cash reserves as the Members shall deem necessary or advisable, including, but not limited to reserves for capital expenditures, replacements, contingent or unforeseen liabilities or other obligations of the Company.

    7. "Code" means the United States Internal Revenue Code of 1986, as amended. References to specific Code Sections or Treasury

Regulations shall be deemed to refer to such Code Sections or Treasury Regulations as they may be amended from time to time or to any successor Code Sections or Treasury Regulations if the Code Section or Treasury Regulation referred to is repealed.

8. "Company" means the [company name], LLC governed by the Agreement.

9. "Company Property" means all the real and personal property owned by the Company.

10. "Deemed Capital Account" means a Member's Capital Account, as calculated from time to time, adjusted by (i) adding thereto the sum of (A) the amount of such Member's Mandatory Obligation, if any, and (B) each Member's share of Minimum Gain (determined after any decreases therein for such year) and (ii) subtracting therefrom (A) allocations of losses and deductions which are reasonably expected to be made as of the end of the taxable year to the Members pursuant to Code Section 704(e)(2), Code Section 706(d) and Treasury Regulation Section 1.751-1(b)(2)(ii), and (B) distributions which at the end of the taxable year are reasonably expected to be made to the Member to the extent that said distributions exceed offsetting increases to the Member's Capital Account (including allocations of the Qualified Income Offset pursuant to Section 7.4 but excluding allocations of Minimum Gain Charge back pursuant to Section 7.3) that are reasonably expected to occur during (or prior to) the taxable years in which such distributions are reasonably expected to be made.

1. "Interest" or "Company Interest" means the ownership interest of a Member in the Company at any particular time, including the right of such Member to any and all benefits to which such Member may be entitled as provided in the Agreement and in the Act, together with the obligations of such Member to comply with all the terms and provisions of the Agreement and the Act.

12. "Mandatory Obligation" means the sum of (i) the amount of a Member's remaining contribution obligation (including the amount of any Capital Account deficit such Member is obligated to restore upon liquidation) provided that such contribution must be made in all events within ninety (90) days of liquidation of the Member's interest as determined under Treasury Regulation Section 1.704-1(b)(2)(ii)(g) and (ii) the additional amount, if any, such Member would be obligated to contribute as of year end to retire recourse indebtedness of the Company if the Company were to liquidate as of such date and dispose of all of its assets at book value.

13. "Member(s)" means those persons who execute a counterpart of this Agreement and those persons who are hereafter admitted as Members under Section 10.4 below.

14. "Minimum Gain" means the amount determined by computing, with respect to each non-recourse liability of the Company, the amount of gain, if any, that would be realized by the Company if it disposed of the Company Property subject to such non-recourse liability in full satisfaction thereof in a taxable transaction, and then by aggregating the amounts so determined. Such gain shall be determined in accordance with Treasury Regulation Section 1.704-2(d). Each Member's share of Minimum Gain at the end of any taxable year of the Company shall be

determined in accordance with Treasury Regulation Section 1.704-2(g)(1).

15. "Net Income" or "Net Loss" means taxable income or loss (including items requiring separate computation under Section 702 of the Code) of the Company as determined using the method of accounting chosen by the Members and used by the Company for federal income tax purposes, adjusted in accordance with Treasury Regulation Section 1.704-1(b)(2)(iv)(g), for any property with differing tax and book values, to take into account depreciation, depletion, amortization and gain or loss as computed for book purposes.

16. "Percentage Interest" means the percentage interest of each Member as set forth in Section 6.1.

17. "Substitute Member" means an Assignee who has been admitted to all of the rights of membership pursuant to Section 10.4 below.

2. **Name and Formation.**

1 **Name.** The name of the Company shall be [name of company], LLC.

Formation. The Members hereby agree to form and operate the Company under the terms and conditions set forth herein. Except as otherwise provided herein, the rights and liabilities of the Members shall be governed by the Act.

Defects as to Formalities. A failure to observe any formalities or requirements of this Agreement, the Certificate of Formation for the Company or the Act shall not be grounds for imposing personal liability on the Members for liabilities of the Company.

No Partnership Intended for Nontax Purposes. The Members have formed the Company under the Act, and expressly do not intend hereby to form a partnership under either the [state] Act or the [state] Uniform Revised Limited Partnership Act or a corporation under the [state] Business Corporation Act. The Members do not intend to be partners one to another, or partners as to any third party. The Members hereto agree and acknowledge that the Company is to be treated as a partnership for federal income tax purposes.

Rights of Creditors and Third Parties. This Agreement is entered into among the Company and the Members for the exclusive benefit of the Company, its Members and their successors and assigns. The Agreement is expressly not intended for the benefit of any creditor of the Company or any other person. Except and only to the extent provided by applicable statute, no such creditor or third party shall have any rights under the Agreement or any agreement between the Company and any Member with respect to any contribution or otherwise.

Title to Property. All Company property shall be owned by the Company as an entity and no Member shall have any ownership interest in such property in the Member's individual name or right, and each Member's interest in the Company shall be personal property for all purposes. Except as otherwise provided in this Agreement, the Company shall hold all Company property in the name of the Company and not in the name or names of any Member or Members.

      Payments of Individual Obligations. The Company's credit and assets shall be used solely for the benefit of the Company, and no asset of the Company shall be transferred or encumbered for or in payment of any individual obligation of any Member unless otherwise provided for herein.

    3.   **Office; Registered Agent.** The principal office of the Company shall be at [address] or at such other place designated by the Members. The agent for service of process for the Company shall be [name of agent for company] at the above address.

    4.   **Term.** The term of the Company shall commence on the filing of the Certificate of Formation, and shall continue until December 31, 2021, unless sooner terminated in accordance with the provisions of this Agreement and the Act.

    5.   **Purpose and Powers.**

        1   **Purpose.** The purpose of the Company shall be to [state purpose of the business here]. The Company shall have no other purpose without the unanimous consent of the Members.

        2   **Powers.** Subject to the provisions of this Agreement, the Company shall have the following powers:

        To conduct and operate the business of the Company and to execute documents and instruments relating to the Company business, including, but not limited to, notes, mortgages, deeds of trust, leases, management agreements, contracts and other documents.

        To procure and maintain insurance covering the various risks to which the Company or its operations may be subject.

        To open bank accounts in the name of the Company, designate the authorized signatures therefor and make deposits and withdrawals from Company accounts on the signatures of one or more designated individuals.

        To pay expenses incurred in performing the business and purposes of the Company.

        To do all things necessary, incidental or convenient to the exercise of the foregoing powers and to the accomplishment of the foregoing purposes.

    6   **Percentage Interests and Capital Contributions.**

        1   **Percentage Interests.** The Members shall have the Percentage Interests in the Company as set forth opposite each Member's name below:

Member	Percentage Interest
[Name]	[percentage]
[Name]	[percentage]

The Percentage Interest of the Members shall be subject to adjustment as provided in Section 6.3.

2   Initial Capital Contributions. Upon execution of this Agreement, the Members will contribute the aggregate amount of [amount of initial investment here] pro rated by percentage. The Members agree that any expenditures made to date with respect to the business by the Members shall be deemed to be Capital Contributions to the Company, and the Member who made such expenditure shall receive a credit to his/her or its Capital Account for such expenditure.

3   Additional Capital Contributions. If the Company requires funds from time to time in excess of the Initial Capital Contributions provided for in Section 6.2, the Members by Percentage Interest shall contribute such amounts in cash as additional Capital Contributions to the Company when required.

In the event either Member fails to contribute its share of capital to the Company (the "Non-Contributing Member"), then the other Member ("Contributing Member") who has contributed its share may at its option:

Treat the Non-Contributing Member as a Defaulting Member under Section 11;

Contribute the amount required from the Non-Contributing Member and elect to readjust the Percentage Interests of the Members in the Company so that the Percentage Interest of each Member is in the ratio of a fraction, the numerator of which is the aggregate Capital Contributions of each Member pursuant to this Section 6.3 and Section 6.2, and the denominator of which is the aggregate Capital Contributions of both Members pursuant to this Section 6.3 and Section 6.2; or

Advance the Non-Contributing Member's pro rata share to the Company and treat such amount as a loan from the Contributing Member to the Non-Contributing Member (a "Default Loan"). Such Default Loans shall bear interest at a rate equal to [prime rate or other such published rate] in effect as of the first day of the calendar month for the month the Default Loan is made, which rate may be adjusted prospectively thereafter as of the first day of each calendar month. Default Loans shall be repayable within thirty (30) days after written demand, and if not sooner repaid or demand made, shall be repaid from any distributions of Cash Available for Distribution otherwise to be made to the Non-Contributing Member by the Company or offset against any amount to be paid to the Non-Contributing Member in purchase of its interest in the Company.

4   No Interest on Capital Contributions. No interest shall be paid on any Capital Contribution Contributions or Capital Accounts of the Members.

5   Capital Accounts. The Company shall establish and maintain a Capital Account for each Member in accordance with Treasury Regulations issued under Code Section 704. The initial Capital Account balance for each Member shall be the amount of initial Capital Contributions made by each Member under Section 6.2 above. The Capital Account of each Member shall be increased to reflect (i) such Member's cash contributions, (ii) the fair market value of property contributed by such Member (net of liabilities securing such contributed property that the Company

is considered to assume or take subject to under Code Section 752), (iii) such Member's share of Net Income (including all gain as calculated pursuant to Section 1001 of the Code) of the Company and (iv) such Member's share of income and gain exempt from tax. The Capital Account of each Member shall be reduced to reflect (a) the amount of money and the fair market value of property distributed to such Member (net of liabilities securing such distributed property that the Member is considered to assume or take subject to under Section 752), (b) such Member's share of non-capitalized expenditures not deductible by the Company in computing its taxable income as determined under Code Section 705(a)(2)(B), (c) such Member's share of Net Loss of the Company and (d) such Member's share of amounts paid or incurred to organize the Company or to promote the sale of Company Interests to the extent that an election under Code Section 709(b) has not properly been made for such amounts. The Members shall determine the fair market value of all property which is distributed in kind, and the Capital Accounts of the Members shall be adjusted as though the property had been sold for its fair market value and the gain or loss attributable to such sale allocated among the Members in accordance with Section 12.3, as applicable. In the event of a contribution of property with a fair market value which is not equal to its adjusted basis (as determined for federal income tax purposes), a revaluation of the Members' Capital Accounts upon the admission of new members to the Company, or in other appropriate situations as permitted by Treasury Regulations issued under Code Section 704, the Company shall separately maintain "tax" Capital Accounts solely for purposes of taking into account the variation between the adjusted tax basis and book value of Company property in tax allocations to the Members consistent with the principles of Code Section 704(c) in accordance with the rules prescribed in Treasury Regulations promulgated under Code Section 704.

7. Allocations.

1 Allocation of Net Income and Net Loss from Operations. Except as otherwise provided in this Section 7 and Section 12, the Company shall allocate Net Income and Net Loss to the Members in proportion to each Member's Percentage Interest.

Limitation on Net Loss Allocations. Notwithstanding anything contained in this Section 7, no Member shall be allocated Net Loss to the extent such allocation would cause a negative balance in such Member's Deemed Capital Account as of the end of the taxable year to which such allocation relates.

Minimum Gain Charge back. If there is a net decrease in Minimum Gain during a taxable year of the Company, then notwithstanding any other provision of this Section 7 or Section 12, each Member must be allocated items of income and gain for such year, and succeeding taxable years to the extent necessary (the "Minimum Gain Charge back"), in proportion to, and to the extent of, an amount required under Treasury Regulation Section 1.704-2(f).

Qualified Income Offset. If at the end of any taxable year and after operation of Section 7.3, any Member shall have a negative balance in such Member's Deemed Capital Account, then notwithstanding anything contained in this Section 7, there shall be reallocated to each Member with a negative balance in such Member's Deemed Capital Account (determined after the allocation of income, gain or loss under this

Section 7 for such year) each item of Company gross income (unreduced by any deductions) and gain in proportion to such negative balances until the Deemed Capital Account for each such Member is increased to zero.

Curative Allocations. The allocations set forth in Sections 7.2, 7.3 and 7.4 (the "Regulatory Allocations") are intended to comply with certain requirements of the Treasury Regulations issued pursuant to Code Section 704(b). It is the intent of the Members that, to the extent possible, all Regulatory Allocations shall be offset either with other Regulatory Allocations or with special allocations of other items of Company income, gain, loss, or deduction pursuant to this Section 7.5. Therefore, notwithstanding any other provision of this Section 7 (other than the Regulatory Allocations), the Members shall make such offsetting special allocations of Company income, gain, loss, or deduction in whatever manner they determine appropriate so that, after such offsetting allocations are made, each Member's Capital Account balance is, to the extent possible, equal to the Capital Account balance such Member would have had if the Regulatory Allocations were not part of the Agreement and all Company items were allocated pursuant to Section 7.1.

Deficit Capital Accounts at Liquidation. It is understood and agreed that one purpose of the provisions of this Section 7 is to insure that none of the Members has a deficit Capital Account balance after liquidation and to insure that all allocations under this Section 7 will be respected by the Internal Revenue Service. The Members and the Company neither intend nor expect that any Member will have a deficit Capital Account balance after liquidation and, notwithstanding anything to the contrary in this Agreement, the provisions of this Agreement shall be construed and interpreted to give effect to such intention. However, if following a liquidation of a Member's interest as determined under Treasury Regulation Section 1.704-1(b)(2)(ii)(g), a Member has a deficit balance in such Member's Capital Account after the allocation of Net Income pursuant to this Section 7 and Section 12 and all other adjustments have been made to such Member's Capital Account for Company operations and liquidation, no Member shall have any obligation to restore such deficit balance.

8. Distributions of Cash Available for Distribution. At such times and in such amounts as the Members determine appropriate, Cash Available for Distribution shall be distributed among the Members in proportion to their Percentage Interests.

9. Management and Accounting.

1 Management. All management decisions or other matters affecting the Company shall be made by unanimous agreement of the Members. To assist in the administration of the business of the Company, the Members may from time to time designate an Administrative Member as the Member responsible for the day-to-day operations of the Company. The Administrative Member is authorized to operate and manage the day-to-day business and affairs of the Company in accordance with this Agreement and shall be the "Tax Matters Partner" of the Company as that term is defined in Internal Revenue Code section 6231(a)(7). The initial Administrative Member shall be [name of Administrative Member].

The Administrative Member shall receive no salary or fees from the Company, but may be reimbursed for expenses in connection with the management of the affairs of the Company.

2.   Accounting. The books and records of the Company shall be kept, and federal income tax returns shall be filed in accordance with federal income tax accounting principles applied on a consistent basis from year to year. The fiscal year of the Company shall be the calendar year. All books and records of the Company shall be open at all times for inspection by either Member.

10.   Transfers.

Transfer Prohibited. No Member may directly or indirectly sell, transfer, assign, pledge or otherwise encumber, voluntarily or involuntarily, all or any part of its interest in the Company without the written consent of the other Member or as provided in Section 10.3, and any other transfer or encumbrance shall be void.

Withdrawal.   A Member shall have no right to withdraw from the Company.

Right of First Refusal. A Member may sell its interest in the Company upon compliance with the following conditions:

In the event a Member ("Selling Member") desires to sell its interest in the Company and receives a written offer ("Offer") therefor which the Selling Member intends to accept, the Selling Member before accepting such Offer shall first notify the other Member ("Non-Selling Member") and provide him with a copy of the Offer. The Offer must contain all material terms relating to the purchase and sale (including the name of the transferee), the consideration must be entirely monetary, and the Offer must contain a provision that the transferee agrees to be bound by all the terms and conditions of this Agreement.

After receiving a copy of the Offer, the Non-Selling Member shall have sixty (60) days within which to elect to purchase the interest of the Selling Member upon the terms and conditions set forth in the Offer. If the Non-Selling Member does not respond or does not elect to purchase the interest of the Selling Member within sixty (60) days, the Selling Member may effect the purchase and sale to the purchaser identified in the Offer and upon the terms and conditions set forth in the Offer, but not otherwise.

In the event the Non-Selling Member elects to purchase the interest of the Selling Member, the Non-Selling Member shall close the purchase and sale within the time period set forth in the Offer or within sixty (60) days after receipt of the Offer, whichever is later.

Admission of Transferee as Member.

No transferee of a Member shall be admitted as a Member unless all of the following conditions have been satisfied:

(i)   The transfer complies with Sections 10.1 or 10.3;

(ii)   The written consent of the

Members to such transferee being admitted as a Member is first obtained, which consent may be arbitrarily withheld;

(iii) The prospective transferee has executed an instrument, in form and substance satisfactory to the Members, accepting and agreeing to be bound by all the terms and conditions of this Agreement and has paid all expenses of the Company in effecting the transfer;

(iv) All requirements of the Act regarding the admission of a transferee Member have been complied with by the transferee, the transferring Member and the Company; and

(v) Such transfer is effected in compliance with all applicable state and federal securities laws.

5 Buy-Sell in Event of Deadlock. If the Members are unable to agree concerning the affairs of the Company for a period of thirty (30) days after either Member declares a deadlock in writing, then either Member may proceed as follows:

The Member declaring the deadlock ("Initiating Member") shall provide to the other Member (the "Non-Initiating Member") a written notice of its intention to invoke the provisions of this section together with a price for all the assets of the Company ("Price Notice").

The Non-Initiating Member within thirty (30) days after receipt of the written notice and the Price Notice provided for in subsection 10.4(a) must elect to either: (i) purchase the interest of the Initiating Member in the Company for the amount the Initiating Member would have received had the assets of the Company been sold for the price specified in the Price Notice, the liabilities of the Company satisfied, and the assets of the Company distributed in cash as provided in Section 12; or (ii) sell its interest to the Initiating Member for the amount the Non-Initiating Member would have received had the assets of the Company been sold for the price specified in the Price Notice, the liabilities of the Company satisfied, and the assets of the Company distributed in cash as provided in Section 12.

The purchase and sale shall close within thirty (30) days after the Non-Initiating Member has notified the Initiating Member of its election pursuant to subsection 10.4(b). If the Initiating Member or the Non-Initiating Member fails to purchase and sell in accordance with the election pursuant to subsection 10.5(b), it shall be a Defaulting Member as defined in Section 11.

A Member who is a Defaulting Member as defined in Section 11 may not invoke the provisions of this Section 10.5.

6 Purchase of Defaulting Member's Interest. In the event either Member shall be a Defaulting Member, the other Member (the "Non-Defaulting Member") may elect to purchase the interest of the Defaulting Member in the Company upon the following terms:

The Non-Defaulting Member shall notify the Defaulting Member of its election to purchase the Defaulting Member's interest and along with such notice shall designate an MAI appraiser who shall establish within twenty (20) days thereafter the appraised fair market value of the Company's assets. Goodwill of the Company, if any, shall not be considered in determining fair market value. The cost of the appraisal shall be charged to the Defaulting Member.

The Non-Defaulting Member shall then purchase the Defaulting Member's interest in the Company for an amount equal to ninety percent (90%) of the amount the Defaulting Member would have received had the assets of the Company been sold for the appraised fair market value determined as provided in subsection 10.5(a), the liabilities of the Company satisfied, and the assets of the Company distributed in cash as provided in Section 12.

The purchase shall close within thirty (30) days after the appraised fair market value is determined as provided in subsection 10.5(a).

7   General Conditions. The Member whose interest is purchased pursuant to Sections 10.2 through 10.5 shall be indemnified by the purchasing Member from any Company liabilities except to the extent any such liabilities were not taken into account in determining the amount the Member would receive pursuant to Section 12. The purchasing Member shall pay the applicable purchase price in cash at closing and the Selling Member shall assign its Company interest and convey by quitclaim deed its interest in the Property to the purchasing Member at closing.

11.   Default.

1   Events of Default. A Member shall be in default ("Defaulting Member") hereunder upon the occurrence of any of the following events:

(a)   If either Member makes an assignment for the benefit of creditors or applies for the appointment of a trustee, liquidator or receiver of any part of its assets or commences any proceedings relating to such Member under any federal or state law relating to bankruptcy, insolvency, reorganization or similar laws;

(b) If either Member has a proceeding commenced against it relating to the appointment of a trustee, liquidator or receiver or pursuant to any proceedings under any federal or state law relating to bankruptcy, insolvency, reorganization or similar laws, which proceeding is not dismissed within ninety (90) days after the filing of such proceeding;

(c)   If either Member suffers its Interest in the Company to become subject to any attachment, levy, execution or other judicial seizure;

(d)   If either Member fails to make a Capital Contribution to the Company as provided in Section 6.3;

(e) If either Member transfers its Interest in violation of Section 10;

(f) If either Member breaches or fails to perform any other provision of this Agreement and such breach or failure is not cured within thirty (30) days after written notice; or

(g) If either Member is judicially determined to be incompetent.

Remedies. Upon either Member becoming a Defaulting Member, the Non-Defaulting Member may:

Dissolve and terminate the Company as provided in Section 12 and offset against any amount to be distributed to the Defaulting Member the damages caused the Company by the Defaulting Member;

Elect to purchase the interest of the Defaulting Member pursuant to Section 10.6;

Exercise the remedies provided in Section 6 for a failure to make a Capital Contribution; or

Pursue any remedy at law or in equity against the Defaulting Member.

A Defaulting Member shall have no right to vote upon or otherwise participate in management of the Company, regardless of whether the Non-Defaulting Member has commenced to exercise any available remedies.

12. Dissolution and Termination.

Dissolution. The Company shall be dissolved upon the occurrence of any of the following events:

Expiration of the term of the Company stated in Section 4 hereof;

Unanimous agreement of the Members;

Sale or disposition of all or substantially all of the Company assets;

Election of the Non-Defaulting Member pursuant to Section 11.2(a); or

The death, incompetence, withdrawal, expulsion, bankruptcy, resignation, or dissolution of a Member, or any other event that terminates the continued membership of such Member unless at the time of the occurrence of any of such event there are at least two other Members, and within 90 days of such occurrence, all remaining Members consent to the continuation of the Company, in which case the business of the Company shall be carried on by the remaining Members.

Neither Member shall have the right to dissolve or terminate the Company for any reason other than as set forth above.

2 Distribution of Cash Upon Termination. If the Company is dissolved pursuant to Section 12.1, the Company affairs shall be wound up

as expeditiously as possible, the assets sold, and the Company terminated. Either Member may be a purchaser of any or all of the assets. After payment of all Company liabilities and expenses of sale and allocations pursuant to Section 12.3, the remaining cash shall be distributed to the Members in accordance with their positive Capital Accounts as adjusted by the allocations provided for in Section 12.3.

There shall be deducted or added to the above, as the case may be, any final adjustments between the Members by reason of Default Loans or offsets as provided in this Agreement.

3 Allocation of Net Income and Net Loss Upon Termination or Sale. All Net Income and Net Loss upon dissolution of the Company or from sale, conversion, disposition or taking of all or substantially all of the Company's property, including, but not limited to the proceeds of any eminent domain proceeding or insurance award (respectively, "Gain on Sale" or "Loss on Sale") shall be allocated as follows:

Loss on Sale shall be allocated between the Members as follows:

First, proportionately to those Members having positive Capital Account balances until all positive Capital Accounts have been reduced to zero; and

Thereafter, to the Members in proportion to their Percentage Interests.

Gain on Sale to the extent available shall be allocated between the Members as follows:

First, proportionately to those Members having negative Capital Account balances until such negative balances are eliminated;

Second, to the Members in such amounts and to the extent necessary, to cause their Capital Account balances to be in proportion to their Percentage Interests; and

(iii) Thereafter, to the Members in proportion to their Percentage Interests.

13. Conflicts of Interest. Each Member understands that the other Member may engage in other business activities which may compete directly or indirectly with the Company, including, but not limited to, the acquisition of other real property or other business activities in the same geographical area. Each Member hereby consents to such other business activities and agrees that no Member shall acquire any interest therein by virtue of this Company.

14. Indemnity and Contribution. Any Member who incurs a Company liability without authority to do so shall indemnify, defend and hold harmless the Company and the other Member against the entire amount of such liability.

15. Notices. Any notice required or permitted under this Agreement

shall be delivered to the address or sent to the facsimile number set forth below each Member's name on the signature page hereof.

16. **Governing Law.** This Agreement shall be governed by the internal laws of the State of [state].

17. **Agreement Binding Upon Successors and Assigns.** This Agreement shall be binding upon the successors and assigns of the Members.

18. **Arbitration.**

1   Any controversy or claim among the Members arising out of or relating to this Agreement including, but not limited to, a claim based on or arising from an alleged tort, will, at the request of any Member be determined by arbitration. The arbitration shall be conducted in accordance with the Federal Arbitration Act (Title 9, U.S. Code), notwithstanding any choice of law provision in this Agreement, and under the Commercial Rules of the American Arbitration Association. The arbitrator(s) shall give effect to statutes of limitation in determining any claim. Any controversy concerning whether an issue is arbitrable shall be determined by the arbitrator(s). The award rendered by the arbitrator(s) shall be final, and the judgment may be entered in any court having jurisdiction thereof. The institution and maintenance of an action for judicial relief or pursuit of a provisional or ancillary remedy shall not constitute a waiver or the right of any Member, including the plaintiff, to submit the controversy or claim to arbitration if any Member contests such action for judicial relief.

In any arbitration proceeding, the arbitrator(s) is(are) authorized to apportion costs and expenses, including investigation, legal and other expense, which will include, if applicable, a reasonable estimate of allocated costs and expenses or in-house legal counsel and legal staff. Such costs and expenses are to be awarded only after the conclusion of the arbitration and will not be advanced during the course of such arbitration.

19. **Amendments.** Except as otherwise provided by law, this Agreement may be amended in any respect with the written consent of both Members.

20. **Counterparts.** This Agreement may be executed in any number of counterparts and by different parties hereto in separate counterparts, each of which when so executed shall be deemed to be an original and all of which when taken together shall constitute one and the same agreement. Delivery of any executed counterpart of a signature page to this Agreement by facsimile shall be effective as delivery of an executed original counterpart of this Agreement.

21. **Pronouns and Paragraph Headings.** As required by the context, all pronouns shall be deemed to refer to and include masculine, feminine, neuter, singular, and plural. Paragraph headings shall be inserted solely for the convenience of the Members and shall not be considered a part of this Agreement for interpretation or construction.

22. **Legal Representation - Conflicts of Interest.** Each party hereto recognizes and acknowledges that each such party may have an actual or potential

adverse interest or conflict of interest in relationship to the other parties hereto and that because of such, the law firm of [name of firm involved in partnership] (including its partners, employees, agents and successors) (collectively, "Counsel") may have an actual or potential conflict of interest by representing more than one of the parties hereto, or arising from another representation of a party. All the parties acknowledge that Counsel is representing the Company with respect to this Agreement and the other parties acknowledge that they have been advised to seek independent counsel. Each party to this Agreement also agrees that in the event of a situation arising wherein a party hereto is in an adverse position to another party with respect to this Agreement or otherwise, Counsel may, at its sole and absolute discretion, represent one or more of the parties hereto or the Company and may decline to represent one or more of such parties or the Company.

MEMBERS:

_____   Dated: _____
[name]

_____   Dated: _____
[name]

_____   Dated: _____
[name]

_____   Dated: _____
[name]

Buy-Sell Agreement

This Buy-Sell Agreement ("Agreement"), is entered into on _____ at _____, between _____ a _____ corporation and _____ (collectively, "Shareholders") with regard to all of the Corporation's stock outstanding now or in the future. The Corporation and the Shareholders agree as follows:

Article I. Parties and Purposes
Identity of Parties
1.1. The shareholders named above own all of the outstanding shares of the Corporation.

Protective Purpose of Agreement
1.2 The purpose of this Agreement is to protect the Corporation's management and control from persons not acceptable to all shareholders. The other purpose is to provide a ready market in the event of the death, disability or lifetime transfer of shares by a Shareholder.

Article II. Enforcement
Restriction on Transfer
2.1. To accomplish the purposes of this Agreement, any transfer, sale, assignment of any of the shares of the Corporation, other than according to the terms of this Agreement, is void. Each Shareholder shall have the right to vote shares held of record and to receive dividends paid on them until the shares are sold or transferred in accordance with this Agreement.

Legend on Share Certificates
2.2. Each share certificate whether presently owned or subsequently acquired, shall have the following statement conspicuously printed on its face:

"The transfer, sale, assignment of the shares represented by this certificate is restricted by a Buy-Sell Agreement among all the Shareholders and the Corporation dated _____. A copy of the Buy-Sell Agreement is available for inspection during normal business hours at the principal office of the Corporation. All the terms and provisions of the Buy-Sell Agreement are incorporated by this reference and made a part of this certificate."

Article III Voluntary Lifetime Transfer of Shares
Permitted Transfers
3.01. Each Shareholder has the right to transfer shares to another shareholder. A permitted transferee shall hold the transferred shares subject to all the provisions of this Agreement, as provided in Section 3.07.

Notice of Proposed Sale
3.02. Except as provided in Section 3.01, any Shareholder wishing to sell his/her shares shall provide a Notice of Proposed Sale. The notice must specify:
- the name and address of each proposed transferee
- the number of shares or the interest in shares to be transferred
- the price per share
- the terms of the proposed sale, assignment, or transfer.

Purchase by Remaining Shareholders
3.03. The Remaining Shareholders have the right, but not the obligation, to purchase the offered shares at the price determined by Article 9 of this Agreement. Within 30 days of notification of the Proposed Sale, any Shareholder who chooses shall notify the Secretary of the Corporation of his/her election to purchase a specified number of the offered shares.

Excessive Offers to Purchase

3.04. If the Remaining Shareholders elect to purchase shares in excess of the amount offered, the available shares shall be allocated according to the same proportion as the existing shares owned by those shareholders.

3.05. Within 30 days, the Secretary of the Corporation shall notify the shareholders of the final purchasers of the offered shares. Each shareholder must meet the terms and conditions of the purchase within ten days after the Shareholder receives the Secretary's notification.

Default of Option by Shareholders

3.06. If the Remaining Shareholders do not purchase all of the shares specified in the Notice of Proposed Sale, the selling shareholder may sell them to the proposed transferee specified in the Notice of Proposed Sale on the terms specified in that notice. The transferee will hold the shares subject to the provision of this Agreement. The selling Shareholder may not, however, sell any or all of the offered shares to any other person or firm or at any other price or on any other terms and conditions than those specified in the Notice of Proposed Sale. Any sale or transfer by any Shareholder in violation of this Article 3 shall be null and void.

Obligations of Transferees

3.07. Unless this Agreement expressly provides otherwise, each transferee and any subsequent transferee of the shares of this Corporation, or of any interest in those shares, shall hold the shares or interest subject to the provisions of this Agreementand shall make no transfers except as provided in this Agreement. The Secretary of the Corporation shall record these transfers on the books of the Corporation until an amended copy of this Agreement has been executed by the transferee. The transferee's failure or refusal to sign an amended copy of this Agreementdoes not relieve the transferee of any obligation or restriction under this Agreement.

Article IV Involuntary Lifetime Transfer of Shares

Involuntary Transfer

4.01. If a Shareholder's shares are transferred involuntarily due to bankruptcy or divorce, 60 days after notice of the event, the other Shareholders shall have the option, but not the obligation to purchase all or some of the shares owned by the Shareholder at the price and the terms provided in this Agreement. The option shall be exercisable by the Shareholders, according to the provisions of Article 3. If the option is not exercised with regard to all of the shares owned by the Shareholder, the Shareholder or the Shareholder's successor in interest will hold the remaining shares subject to this Agreement.

Article V- Sale of Shares on Death

Purchase by Surviving Shareholders

5.01. Within 60 days after the death of any Shareholder, the surviving Shareholders shall, at the price and on the terms and conditions specified in this Agreement, purchase from the Decedent's estate all the shares owned by the decedent. The obligation of the surviving Shareholders to the decedent's estate under this Article shall be joint and several. However, each surviving Shareholder shall have the right and obligation to purchase the available shares in proportion to his or her existing ownership interests – exclusive of the decedent's shares at the date of the decedent's death.

Death of Shareholder's Spouse

5.02 The death of a Shareholder's spouse who has never been active in or devoted his or her full working time to the business of the Corporation shall not be considered the death of a Shareholder for purposes of this Article.

Method of Payment of Purchase Price

5.03 .The purchase price for the decedent's shares shall be paid to the decedent's estate or the decedent's successor in interest in a lump sum. The purchase price of the shares shall be determined in accordance with Article 9.

Article VI. Transfer on Total Disability
Transfer on Disability of Shareholder

6.01. If a Shareholder becomes either physically or mentally disabled for a period of 90 days, and a physician's opinion is issued stating that the disability will continue for one year, the Remaining Shareholders shall have the option, but not the obligation to purchase all of the shares of the disabled Shareholder within 90 days of that notice. The price and terms shall be according to Article 3 of this Agreement. If the option is not exercised with regard to all the shares of the disabled Shareholder, the disabled Shareholder - or the Shareholder's successor in interest - shall hold the shares subject to the provisions of this Agreement.

Article VII. Transfer on Termination of Employment
Termination of Employment

7.01 If the employment of a Shareholder with the Corporation is terminated for any reason, the Remaining Shareholders shall have the option, but not the obligation, within 90 days after receiving notice of the event, to purchase all of the shares of the terminated Shareholder at the price and on the terms provided in this Agreement and in the manner described in Article 3. If the option is not exercised with regard to all the shares of the terminated Shareholder, the Shareholder shall hold the shares subject to the provisions of this Agreement.

Article VIII. Payment for and Transfer of Shares
Delivery and Enforcement of Shares

8.01. The purchaser shall deliver the consideration for the shares as soon as practicable to the selling Shareholder, as well as the endorsed certificates representing the shares for transfer.

Transfer of Title

8.02. On any transfer of shares under this Agreement, title to the shares shall pass from the seller to the purchaser upon payment by the purchaser of the consideration and endorsement of the share certificates by the seller as provided in Section 8.01. The seller's status as a shareholder thereupon shall cease.

Article IX: Determination of Purchase Price.
Purchase Price set by Appraisal

9.01 The purchase price of the shares subject to this Agreement shall be the value of the shares set by appraisal.

Selection of Appraiser

9.02 Within 10 days after an event requiring the determination of purchase price, the Corporation and the selling Shareholder shall mutually select a qualified appraiser to appraise the Corporation and set a value on its stock.

Binding Nature of Determination

9.03 The value of the shares computed according to this Article is binding on all persons.

Article X Termination of Agreement
Events Causing Termination

10.01 This Agreement shall terminate on any the following:
- The written consent of parties to the Agreement.
- The dissolution, bankruptcy, or insolvency of the Corporation.
- One shareholder becoming the owner of all the shares.

Article XI. Miscellaneous Provisions
Amendments

11.01 This Agreement may be amended only by written consent of all parties to the

Agreement.

Notices.

11.02 All notices, demands, request or communications required or permitted by this Agreement shall be in writing and shall be deemed duly served when personally delivered to the party or to an officer or agent of the party, or when deposited in the United States mail, first class postage prepaid, addressed to the corporation at its principal office or to a Shareholder at the address on the books and record the Corporation.

Attorney's Fees.

11.03 In the event of any litigation concerning this Agreement, the prevailing party shall be entitled, in addition to any other relief that may be granted, to reasonable attorney's fees.

Binding on Successors and Assigns.

11.04 This Agreement shall be binding on the parties to the Agreement and on each of their heirs, executors, administrators, successors, and assigns.

Severability

11.05 If any provision is unenforceable or invalid or any reason, the remaining provisions shall be unaffected by such a holding.

Governing Law

11.06 This Agreement shall be construed according to and governed by the laws of the State of _____. However, in the event of death of a shareholder, the purchase price shall be no less than the value of the shares as finally determined for federal estate tax purposes.

Sole Agreement.

11.07 This instrument constitutes the only Agreement of the parties regarding the sale and purchase of their shares in the Corporation and correctly sets forth the rights, duties and obligations of each to the other. Any prior agreements, promises, negotiations or representations concerning the Agreement's subject matter not expressly set forth in this Agreement are of no force or effect.

Agreement Available for Inspection.

11.08 An original copy of this Agreement duly executed by the Corporation and by each of the Shareholders shall be delivered to the Secretary of the Corporation and maintained by the Secretary at the principal office of the Corporation available for inspection by any person requesting to see it.

Executed on

By: _____

Work for Hire, Non-Disclosure and Confidentiality Agreement

This agreement (the "Agreement") is made this ____ day of _____, 20__, between [Company], a [state] corporation (the "Company") and _____, a Limited Liability Company ("Contractor"), and when used together, (the "Parties").

1. The Company hereby engages Contractor to provide services to the Company as an independent contractor going forward (the "Engagement"). The services to be provided will be assigned by the Company to Contractor from time-to-time or as attached on Schedule A.

2. As full and complete compensation for Contractor's services and all rights granted or assigned to the Company by Contractor under this Agreement, the Company will pay Contractor as attached on Schedule B. Payment will be made to Contractor pursuant to form 1099 without deduction for federal or state income tax or any other type of unemployment compensation, social security withholding, or any other tax deduction. The Company shall also reimburse Contractor for all pre-approved out-of-pocket expenses.

3. Contractor represents and warrants to the Company that Contractor is either a sole proprietor or a legal company authorized to do business in the State of Florida, with all licenses and permits that are required to perform the services contemplated herein. Contractor will be solely responsible for the payment of all income tax, social security tax, sales tax, service tax, use tax, license fees, Contractor's license fees, or any other fee, fine, penalty or tax of whatever nature added by or imposed by any federal, state or local governmental agency or authority with regard to the performance of services to the Company and compensation derived therefrom by Contractor.

4. The parties hereto intend and acknowledge that they are "independent contractors," and nothing in this Agreement shall be construed to create an employer/employee, partnership, fiduciary or joint venture relationship. Contractor will indemnify and hold the Company harmless from any and all loss or liability arising with respect to such payments, withholdings, and benefits, if any and Contractor shall not take the position that he is an employee of the Company in any proceeding in front of any court of law, tribunal, administrative panel or otherwise, nor shall he assert any claim or initiate any action against the Company in which he contends he acted as an "employee" of the Company in connection with the performance of services on behalf of the Company.

5. Contractor shall not hold himself out as having any right, power or authority to create any contract or obligation, either expressed or implied, on behalf of, or in the name of, or binding upon the Company. Contractor, as an independent contractor, shall not be covered by any health, worker's compensation, or disability insurance plans of the Company, shall not be entitled to any fringe benefits normally provided by the Company for its employees and shall not receive pay for vacations or holidays. Further, Contractor expressly waives and voluntary elects to be exempt from coverage under the {State} Worker's Compensation Act. Contractor acknowledges and agrees that the

Company does not guarantee a specific hourly rate or average amount of revenue/pay. Contractor retains full control and discretion on any services it performs for the Company, and retains full control and discretion on the number of hours Contractor chooses to work, and retains full control and discretion on the hours and days Contractor chooses to work; and thus retains full discretion on the potential revenue Contractor may or may not generate under this Agreement.

6. The work product of Contractor's services provided pursuant to this Agreement, including the services previously performed, is the "Work." To the extent that the Work includes any material subject to copyright that Work is done as and constitutes a "work for hire" as defined under U.S. and all other relevant copyright laws to the fullest extent permitted, and as a result the Company shall own all copyrights in and to such Work. To the extent that the Work includes any material subject to copyright which is not "work for hire," or is subject to patent, trade secret, or other intellectual property protection, Contractor hereby irrevocably assigns, transfers and conveys to the Company, and its successors and assigns, all right, title and interest in and to the Work, including all copyrights, patents, trade secrets, and other intellectual property rights therein (including extensions and renewals thereof and the right to license and assign). Contractor shall execute and deliver such instruments and take such other actions as may be required and requested by Company to carry out the assignment made pursuant to this section. Contractor hereby waives any so-called "droit moral" rights, "moral rights of authors" and all other similar rights however denominated throughout the world. The Company shall not be obligated to either exercise any of the rights granted to the Company herein, make any use of any of the Work, or attribute the Work to Contractor.

7. Contractor represents and warrants that (a) Contractor has the full power and authority to enter into and to fulfill the terms of this Agreement and to grant the rights described herein; (b) Contractor has not entered and will not enter into any agreements or activities that will or might interfere or conflict with the terms hereof; (c) the Work is and will be wholly original with Contractor and not copied in whole or in part from any other work except materials in the public domain or supplied to Contractor by Company; and (d) neither the Work nor the use thereof infringes upon or violates any right of privacy or publicity of, or constitutes a libel, slander or any unfair competition against, or infringes upon or violates the copyright, trademark rights or other intellectual property rights of any person or entity.

8. Contractor agrees to perform, during and after the Engagement, all acts deemed necessary or desirable by Company to permit and assist it, at the Company's expense, in evidencing, perfecting, obtaining, maintaining, defending and enforcing the inventions and intellectual property rights. Contractor hereby irrevocably designates and appoints the Company and its duly authorized officers and agents, as his attorneys-in-fact, with full power of substitution, to act for and on their behalf and instead of me, to execute and file any documents and to do all other lawfully permitted acts to further the above purposes with the same legal force and effect as if executed by Contractor.

9. In the event of an actual or alleged breach of this Agreement by the Company, or under any other circumstances whatsoever, any rights and remedies Contractor may have against the Company or its successors or assigns will be limited to the right to recover damages, if any, in an action at law. Contractor hereby waives any right or remedy in equity, including but not limited to any right to rescind or terminate the

Company's rights hereunder or to seek or obtain injunctive relief of any kind.

10. The Company may disclose to Contractor certain confidential or proprietary information including information relating to its respective past, current or future finances, strategies, business plans, operations, systems, technologies, products and services, (its "Confidential Information") for mutually beneficial purposes. Disclosure of Confidential Information may be in any audible, visible or any other tangible or intangible form or medium, including written, printed, optical, magnetic or electronic.

(a) Contractor shall maintain the confidentiality of the Company's Confidential Information and not disclose such Confidential Information to any third party other than those of its officers, employees and agents who have a reasonable need to know such information for the purposes authorized by the Company and who agree to be bound by the terms of this Non-Disclosure Agreement to the same extent as Contractor.

(b) Contractor shall take precautions which are reasonable, necessary and appropriate to guard the confidentiality of the Company's Confidential Information and shall treat such Confidential Information with at least the same degree of care which it applies to its own confidential and proprietary information.

(c) All Confidential Information is and shall at all times remain the property of the Company. No use of such Confidential Information is permitted except as authorized by the Company and no grant under any of the Company's intellectual property rights is hereby given or intended including any license, implied or otherwise.

(d) Confidential Information does not include any information which the Contractor already had in its possession without confidential limitation at the time of disclosure by the Company; information which is independently developed by the Contractor; information known or that becomes known to the general public without breach of this Agreement by the Contractor; information that is received rightfully and without confidential limitation by the Contractor from a third party; and information which is lawfully required to be disclosed, provided that before making disclosure, the Contractor must where possible give written notice to the Company.

11. In the event of a breach or threatened breach of the terms of this Agreement by Contractor, the Company shall be entitled to seek an injunction in addition to and not in lieu of any other legal or equitable relief including money damages. The parties acknowledge that Confidential Information may be valuable and unique and that disclosure may result in irreparable injury to the Company.

12. Contractor may not assign this Agreement or its rights hereunder, or delegate its obligations hereunder, in whole or in part. The Company may assign this Agreement or any or all of its rights hereunder to any person or entity. All of the Company's affiliates shall be third party beneficiaries of this Agreement.

13. In the event that any provision of this Agreement is determined to be invalid or unenforceable by any court of competent jurisdiction, such determination shall in no way affect or limit the validity or enforceability of the remainder of this Agreement.

14. This Agreement shall be construed under and by the laws of the State of _____. The Parties consent to the exclusive personal jurisdiction and venue of the State and Federal

Courts located in Sarasota County in the State of Florida in any legal action or proceeding brought to enforce, construe or interpret this Agreement. THE PARTIES VOLUNARILY WAIVE ANY RIGHT TO A JURY TRIAL FOR ANY MATTER ARISING OUT OF OR RELATED TO THIS AGREEMENT.

15. Unless otherwise set forth in writing, the Engagement is terminable at will by either party upon written notice. Upon such termination, Contractor shall promptly return to the Company all embodiments of the Confidential Information.

16. The Company's rights and Contractor's obligations under this Agreement shall be deemed to have commenced upon the commencement of the discussions between Contractor and the Company which led to the Engagement by the Company (and the consideration for the application of this Agreement shall be the continuation of the Engagement after the date hereof) and shall survive termination of this Agreement for an indefinite period.

DATED the date first above written.

Contractor: Company:

_____   _____
Signature   Signature

_____   _____
Fed Tax ID Number   Fed Tax ID Number

Schedule A Contractor Services

Contractor shall perform services as _____ for Company, including:

Schedule B Contractor Compensation

Contractor shall be compensated accordingly: _____

Executive Summary Format

Company purpose - Define the company/business in a single declarative sentence.

Problem - Describe the pain of the customer (or the customer's customer). - Outline how the customer addresses the issue today.

Solution - Demonstrate your company's value proposition to make the customer's life better. - Show where your product physically sits. - Provide use cases.

Why now - Set up the historical evolution of your category. - Define recent trends that make your solution possible.

Market size - Identify/profile the customer you cater to. - Calculate the TAM (top down), SAM (bottoms up), and SOM.

Competition - List competitors - List competitive advantages

Product - Product line-up (form factor, functionality, features, architecture, intellectual property). - Development roadmap

Business model - Revenue model - Pricing - Average account size and/or lifetime value - Sales and distribution model - Customer/pipeline list

Team - Founders and management - Board of Directors/Board of Advisors

Financials - P&L - Balance sheet - Cash flow - Cap table - The deal

Intellectual Property Assignment Agreement

(Confidentiality, Invention Assignment, Non-raiding and Noncompetition)

I, the undersigned employee/contractor, agree as follows for the benefit of [Company], Inc., its parents, subsidiaries and affiliates (collectively "[Company]"):

1. <u>Confidentiality</u>. I agree that information that is not generally known to the public to which I have been or will be exposed as a result of my being employed by [Company] is confidential information that belongs to [Company]. This includes information developed by me, alone or with others, or entrusted to [Company] by its customers or others. I will hold [Company]'s confidential information in strict confidence, and not disclose or use it except as authorized by [Company] and for [Company]'s benefit. If anyone tries to compel me to disclose any of [Company]'s confidential information, by subpoena or otherwise, I will immediately notify [Company] so that [Company] may take any actions it deems necessary to protect its interests. My agreements to protect [Company]'s confidential information apply both while I am employed by [Company] and after my employment by [Company] ends, regardless of the reason it ends.

[Company]'s confidential information includes, without limitation, information relating to [Company]'s trade secrets, research and development, product development plans, inventions, know-how, software (including source code and object code), procedures, manufacturing, engineering, purchasing, accounting, marketing, sales, customers, suppliers, financial status or employees.

I understand that this agreement does not limit my right to use my own general knowledge and experience, whether or not gained while employed by [Company], or my right to use information that is or becomes generally known to the public through no fault of my own, but I have the burden in any dispute of showing that information is not [Company]'s confidential information.

I understand it is [Company]'s policy not to improperly obtain or use confidential, proprietary or trade secret information that belongs to third parties, including others who have employed or engaged me or who have entrusted confidential information to me. I will not use for [Company]'s benefit or disclose to [Company] confidential, proprietary or trade secret information that belongs to others, unless I advise [Company] that the information belongs to a third party and both [Company] and the owners of the information consent to the disclosure and use.

2. <u>Inventions, Copyrights and Patents</u>. [Company] owns all Inventions and Works I make, conceive, develop, discover, reduce to practice or fix in a tangible medium of expression, alone or with others, either (a) during my employment by [Company] (including past employment, and whether or not during working hours), or (b) within one year after my employment ends if the Invention or Work results from any work I performed for [Company] or involves the use or assistance of [Company]'s facilities, materials, personnel or confidential information. [Company] also owns all

Inventions and Works of mine that I bring to [Company] that are used in the course of [Company]'s business or that are incorporated into any Inventions or Works that belong to [Company].

I will promptly disclose to [Company], will hold in trust for [Company]'s sole benefit, will assign to [Company] and hereby do assign to [Company] all Inventions and Works described in the prior paragraph, including all copyrights (including renewal rights), patent rights and trade secret rights, vested and contingent. I will waive and hereby do waive any moral rights I have or may have in the Inventions and Works described in the prior paragraph. I agree that all Works I produce within the scope of my employment (which shall include all Works I produce related to [Company]'s business, whether or not done during regular working hours) shall be considered "works made for hire" so that [Company] will be considered the author of the Works under the federal copyright laws. At [Company]'s direction and expense I will execute all documents and take all actions necessary or convenient for [Company] to document, obtain, maintain or assign its rights to these Inventions and Works. [Company] shall have full control over all applications for patents or other legal protection of these Inventions and Works.

"Inventions" means discoveries, developments, concepts, ideas, improvements to existing technology, processes, procedures, machines, products, compositions of matter, formulas, algorithms, computer programs and techniques, and all other matters ordinarily intended by the word "invention," whether or not patentable or copyrightable. "Inventions" also includes all records and expressions of those matters. "Works" means original works of authorship, including interim work product, modifications and derivative works, and all similar matters, whether or not copyrightable.

I understand that this agreement does not apply to any Invention or Work of mine for which no equipment, supplies, facilities or trade secret information of [Company] was used and which was developed entirely on my own time, unless (a) the Invention or Work relates (i) directly to [Company]'s business or (ii) to [Company]'s actual or demonstrably anticipated research or development, or (b) the Invention or Work results from any work I performed for [Company].

3. [Company] Materials. I will safeguard and return to [Company] when my employment ends, or sooner if [Company] requests, all documents and property in my care, custody or control relating to my employment or [Company]'s business, including without limitation any documents that contain [Company]'s confidential information.

4. Nonraiding of Employees. So long as I am employed by [Company] and for twenty-four (24) months after my employment ends, regardless of the reason it ends, I will not directly or indirectly solicit any employee to leave his or her employment with [Company]. This includes that I will not (a) disclose to any third party the names, backgrounds or qualifications of any [Company] employees or otherwise identify them as potential candidates for employment; (b) personally or through any other person approach, recruit or otherwise solicit employees of [Company] to work for any other employer; or (c) participate in any pre-employment interviews with any person who was employed by [Company] while I was employed by [Company].

5. **No Disparagement or Interference**. I will not disparage [Company] or its business or products and will not interfere with [Company]'s relationships with its customers, employees, vendors, bankers or others. This applies both while I am employed by [Company] and after my employment by [Company] ends, regardless of the reason it ends.

6. **Other Employment While Employed By [Company]**. While I am employed by [Company] I will not do work that competes with or relates to any of [Company]'s products or activities without first obtaining [Company]'s written permission. Any business opportunities related to [Company]'s business that I learn of or obtain while employed by [Company] (whether or not during working hours) belong to [Company], and I will pursue them only for [Company]'s benefit.

7. **Noncompetition After Employment by [Company] Ends**. For twenty-four (24) months after my employment by [Company] ends, regardless of the reason it ends, I will not, directly or indirectly: (a) sell, market or propose to sell or market products that compete or will compete with [Company]'s then existing or reasonably anticipated products ("Competing Products") in any geographic area where [Company]'s products are then marketed, (b) design or develop Competing Products, or (c) work for or with, or provide services or information to, any person or entity that (i) sells, markets or proposes to sell or market Competing Products in any geographic area where [Company]'s products are then marketed, (ii) is designing or developing Competing Products, or (iii) is shown on the attached list of Competing Companies.

The persons and entities (other than myself) that are covered by this noncompetition provision are referred to as the "Competing Companies." [Company] maintains a list (the "List") of examples of Competing Companies. A copy of the current List is attached as <u>Exhibit A</u>. The List contains examples only, and is not necessarily a complete list of all Competing Companies.

Where a Competing Company has multiple divisions, this noncompetition provision shall apply only to those divisions that are involved with Competing Products, provided that I and the competitor provide written assurances satisfactory to [Company] that the information and work product I provide to other divisions of the competitor will not be shared, directly or indirectly, or intentionally or unintentionally, with the division involved with Competing Products.

I understand that in cases where this noncompetition provision does not apply, I am still subject to all other obligations I have to [Company], including my obligations related to [Company]'s inventions, copyrights and confidential information.

8. **Disclosure of Other Work**. Before I undertake any work for myself or anyone else during my employment by [Company] or within twenty-four (24) months after my employment ends that will involve subject matter related to [Company]'s activities, I will fully disclose the proposed work to [Company].

9. **Reasonableness of Terms**. I acknowledge that the terms of this agreement are reasonably necessary to protect [Company]'s legitimate business interests. I acknowledge that if my employment with [Company] ends my experience and capabilities are such that I can obtain employment that does not violate this agreement, and that an injunction to enforce this agreement will not prevent me from

earning a reasonable livelihood.

10. <u>Future Consulting or Employment for [Company]</u>. If my employment relationship with [Company] ends but [Company] employs me again or engages me as a consultant, then this agreement shall apply to my later employment(s) or engagement(s) unless they follow a period of a year or more during which I was neither employed nor engaged by [Company]. If this agreement becomes applicable to a consulting relationship, the references in this agreement to my employment by [Company] shall be treated, as appropriate, as referring to my consulting relationship with [Company].

11. <u>No Guarantee of Employment</u>. I understand this agreement is not a guarantee of continued employment. My employment is terminable at any time by [Company] or me, with or without cause or prior notice, unless otherwise provided in a written employment agreement.

12. <u>No Conflicting Agreements</u>. I am not a party to any agreements, such as confidentiality or noncompetition agreements, that limit my ability to perform my duties for [Company].

13. <u>Miscellaneous</u>. If I breach this agreement it will cause [Company] irreparable harm. If I breach or threaten to breach this agreement, [Company] will be entitled to injunctive or other equitable relief as well as money damages. If I breach this agreement, I will hold in trust for [Company] all income I receive as a result of the violation. I consent to [Company] notifying anyone to whom I may provide services of the existence and terms of this agreement. In any lawsuit arising out of or relating to this agreement or my employment, including without limitation arising from any alleged tort or statutory violation, the prevailing party shall recover their reasonable costs and attorneys fees, including on appeal. This agreement shall be governed by the internal laws of the state of [State] without giving effect to provisions thereof related to choice of laws or conflict of laws. Venue and jurisdiction of any lawsuit involving this agreement or my employment shall exist exclusively in state and federal courts in [County], [State], unless injunctive relief is sought by [Company] and, in [Company]'s judgment, may not be effective unless obtained in some other venue. If any part of this agreement is held to be unenforceable, it shall not affect any other part. If any part of this agreement is held to be unenforceable as written, it shall be enforced to the maximum extent allowed by applicable law. My obligations under this agreement supplement and do not limit other obligations I have to [Company], including without limitation under the law of trade secrets. This agreement shall be enforceable regardless of any claim I may have against [Company]. This agreement shall survive the termination of my employment, however caused. The waiver of any breach of this agreement or failure to enforce any provision of this agreement shall not waive any later breach. This agreement is binding on me, my heirs, executors, personal representatives, successors and assigns, and benefits [Company] and its successors and assigns. This agreement is the final and complete expression of my agreement on these subjects, and may be amended only in a writing signed by [Company] and me.

DATED this _____ day of _____, 20__.

EMPLOYEE/CONTRACTOR:

_____
Name: _____[print]

[Company], Inc. _____
ACCEPTANCE: By: _____[print]
_____

Mutual Non-Disclosure Agreement

This Mutual Nondisclosure Agreement (this Agreement), dated as of _____ 20__ is made between _____, a _____ corporation ("Company A"), and _____, a _____ individual/corporation ("Company B"). Company A and Company B would like to exchange information and enter into discussions regarding a possible partnership between them. In connection with that information exchange and those discussions, each party may receive valuable proprietary information relating to the other's ideas, technologies, operations and businesses. Company A and Company B would like to protect the confidentiality of, maintain their respective rights in and prevent the unauthorized use and disclosure of their valuable confidential information. Accordingly, Company A and Company B hereby agree as follows:

1. Confidential Information

As used in this Agreement, (Confidential Information) means all nonpublic information disclosed by one party or its agents (the Disclosing Party) to the other party (the Receiving Party) that is designated as confidential or that, given the nature of the information or the circumstances surrounding its disclosure, reasonably should be considered as confidential. Confidential Information includes, without limitation (i) nonpublic information relating to the Disclosing Party's technology, business plan, customers, promotional and marketing activities, finances and other business affairs, (ii) third-party information that the Disclosing Party is obligated to keep confidential, and (iii) the nature, contents and existence of the parties' negotiations.

2. Exclusions

Confidential Information does not include any information that (i) is or becomes publicly available without breach of this Agreement, (ii) can be shown by documentation to have been known to the Receiving Party at the time of its receipt from the Disclosing Party, (iii) is received from a third party who did not acquire or disclose such information by a wrongful or tortious act, or (iv) can be shown by documentation to have been independently developed by the Receiving Party without reference to any Confidential Information.

3. Use of Confidential Information

The Receiving Party may use Confidential Information only in pursuance of its business relationship with the Disclosing Party. Except as expressly provided in this Agreement, the Receiving Party will not disclose Confidential Information to anyone, or use for its own benefit, without the Disclosing Party's prior written consent. The Receiving Party will take all reasonable measures to avoid disclosure, dissemination or unauthorized use of Confidential Information, including, at a minimum, those measures it takes to protect its own confidential information of a similar nature. The Receiving Party will not export any Confidential Information in any manner contrary to the export regulations of the United States.

4. Receiving Party Personnel

The Receiving Party will restrict the possession, knowledge and use of Confidential Information to its employees, contractors and entities controlled by it who (i) have a need to know Confidential Information in connection with the parties' business relationship, and (ii) have executed written agreements obligating them to protect the Confidential Information.

5. Disclosures to Governmental Entities

The Receiving Party may disclose Confidential Information as required to comply with binding orders of governmental entities that have jurisdiction over it, provided that the Receiving Party (i) gives the Disclosing Party reasonable written notice to allow the Disclosing Party to seek a protective order or other appropriate remedy, (ii) discloses only such information as is required by the governmental entity, and (iii) and uses commercially reasonable efforts to obtain confidential treatment for any Confidential Information so disclosed.

6. Ownership of Confidential Information

All Confidential Information will remain the exclusive property of the Disclosing Party. The Disclosing Party's disclosure of Confidential Information will not constitute an express or implied grant to the Receiving Party of any rights to or under the Disclosing Party's copyrights, trade secrets, trademarks or other intellectual property rights.

7. Notice of Unauthorized Use

The Receiving Party will notify the Disclosing Party immediately upon discovery of any unauthorized use or disclosure of Confidential Information or any other breach of this Agreement by Receiving Party. The Receiving Party will cooperate with the Disclosing Party in every reasonable way to help the Disclosing Party regain possession of such Confidential Information and prevent its further unauthorized use.

8. Return of Confidential Information

The Receiving Party will return or destroy all tangible materials embodying Confidential Information (in any form and including, without limitation, all summaries, copies and excerpts of Confidential Information) promptly following the Disclosing Party's written request. At the Disclosing Party's option, the Receiving Party will provide written certification of its compliance with this Section.

9. Injunctive Relief

The Receiving Party acknowledges that a breach of its obligations under this Agreement could cause irreparable harm to the Disclosing Party for which monetary damages may be difficult to ascertain or an inadequate remedy. The Receiving Party therefore agrees that the Disclosing Party will have the right, in addition to its other rights and remedies, to seek injunctive relief for any violation of this Agreement.

10. Scope; Termination

This Agreement is intended to cover Confidential Information disclosed by each party both prior and subsequent to the date hereof. This Agreement automatically will terminate upon the completion or termination of the parties' business relationship; provided, however, that each party's obligations with respect to the other party's Confidential Information will survive for two years following such completion or termination.

11. Independent Development

The Disclosing Party acknowledges that the Receiving Party may currently or in the future be developing information internally, or receiving information from other parties, that is similar to the Confidential Information. Accordingly, nothing in this Agreement will be construed as a representation or agreement that the Receiving Party will not develop or have developed for it products, concepts, systems or techniques that are similar to or compete with the products, concepts, systems or techniques contemplated by or embodied in the Confidential Information, provided that the Receiving Party does not violate any of its obligations under this Agreement in connection with such development.

12. Miscellaneous

12.1 This Agreement will not create a joint venture, partnership or other formal business relationship or entity of any kind, or an obligation to form any such relationship or entity. Each party will act as an independent contractor and not as an agent of the other party for any purpose, and neither will have the authority to bind the other.

12.2 This Agreement constitutes the entire agreement (and supercedes all previous agreements) between the parties relating to the matters discussed herein and may be amended or modified only with the mutual written consent of the parties. Each party's obligations hereunder are in addition to, and not exclusive of, any and all of its other obligations and duties to the other party, whether express, implied, in fact or in law. Subject to the limitations set forth in this Agreement, this Agreement will inure to the benefit of and be binding upon the parties and their respective successors and assigns.

12.3 Any failure by either party to enforce the other party's strict performance of any provision of this Agreement will not constitute a waiver of its right to subsequently enforce such provision or any other provision of this Agreement.

12.4 If a provision of this Agreement is held invalid under any applicable law, such invalidity will not affect any other provision of this Agreement that can be given effect without the invalid provision. Further, all terms and conditions of this Agreement will be deemed enforceable to the fullest extent permissible under applicable law, and, when necessary, the court is requested to reform any and all terms or conditions to give them such effect.

12.5 This Agreement will be governed by internal laws of the State of _____, without reference to its choice of law rules. Exclusive jurisdiction over and venue of any suit arising out of or relating to this Agreement will be in the state and federal courts of King County, Washington. This Agreement may be executed by facsimile and in counterpart copies.

The parties have executed this Agreement as of the date first written above.

COMPANY A CORPORATION

Name:

Signed:

Title:

COMPANY B

Name:

Signed:

Title:

About the Author

 Michael ODonnell is a serial entrepreneur and startup mentor with 30+ years of experience in starting and building companies backed by angel investors and venture capital. ODonnell founded Data Technologies, Ask-Me Multimedia (acquired by Midisoft), iCopyright.com, Data Depth Corp., and Leaves.com, among other companies. He was on the launch team of CompuServe Sprynet, one of the first national Internet Service Providers (went public as part of CompuServe in 1996), and Design Intelligence (acquired by Microsoft).

ODonnell is the author of two best-selling books on business planning and marketing planning. His book, A True Professional, was published in 2017 to critical acclaim. His 2021 book, Selling A Business Blueprint: Step-by-Step Guide with Forms and Agreements, is a must-read for entrepreneurs planning to sell their businesses.

ODonnell served as Chairman of the Northwest Entrepreneurs Network in Seattle, Washington, one of the largest organizations of entrepreneurs in the country. He was instrumental in bringing The Founder Institute tech accelerator to South Florida and was the director/mentor for two federally funded programs, Startup Quest and StartupNOW. He is an Adjunct Instructor for the Broward College Entrepreneurial Experience (BCEx) and a certified mentor for SCORE. As the founder of StartupBiz.com, ODonnell has assisted more than 25,000 startup members.

ODonnell currently serves as the Managing Partner of SellBiz Mergers and Acquisitions, providing exit planning and business brokerage services to technology companies.

Connect with Mike on LinkedIn at https://www.linkedin.com/in/mikeodonnell/, or email him at mike@startupbiz.com.

About VMT

The Venture Mentoring Team (TheVMT.org) is a nonprofit educational 501(c)(3) dedicated to fostering the startup community by training and credentialing Mentors and then connecting them with the best and brightest entrepreneurs to help startups reach their full potential. We are experienced executives and entrepreneurs in corporate, legal, academic, profit and not for profit organizations that donate our time and talent. Our goal is to help the startups gain sustainability and traction.

www.ingramcontent.com/pod-product-compliance
Lightning Source LLC
Chambersburg PA
CBHW070242220526
45465CB00004B/1490